# THE SPIRITUALITY
## OF THE
## OLD LOW COUNTRIES

# THE SPIRITUALITY
# OF THE
# OLD LOW COUNTRIES

by

STEPHANUS AXTERS, O.P.

*Translated by*

DONALD ATTWATER

1954

BLACKFRIARS PUBLICATIONS

LONDON

First published in English in 1954,
*The Spirituality of the Old Low Countries*
is a translation of *La spiritualité des Pays-
Bas : l'Évolution d'une doctrine mystique*,
published by Editions Nauwelaerts,
Louvain.

*Nihil Obstat :* Hubertus Richards, s.t.l., l.s.s.

*Imprimatur* : E. Morrogh Bernard, Vic. Gen.

*Westmonasterii, die 13a Aprilis, 1954*

*Printed in Great Britain
by The Burleigh Press, Lewins Mead, Bristol*

# CONTENTS

5

# PREFACE

THE following pages are far from being a history of spirituality in the Low Countries: they are in fact a series of conferences which, at the invitation of the directors, I gave in the early summer of 1946 to the Dominican faculties of theology and philosophy at Le Saulchoir, near Paris. The task I undertook was to give a clear and concise sketch of the doctrinal development of Low-Countries spirituality, bringing out whatever constitutes its own characteristics.

The time has certainly not yet come for the making of a synthesis that could be considered definitive. Still, since the publication in 1892 of M. A. Auger's *Étude sur les mystiques des Pays-Bas au moyen âge*—a daring venture that was all to his credit—the state of things has changed a lot. Many hitherto unpublished texts and learned dissertations have seen the light in both Belgium and Holland. Publishing houses in England, France and other countries have issued translations of the chief writings of Ruysbroeck, Thomas a Kempis, Louis de Blois and others. Only a few years ago an octogenarian of the Anglican communion, as he lay dying in an Oxford hospital, spoke to me most feelingly of that "great man", Thomas a Kempis. There is an ever-increasing number of chosen souls who are hungry for holiness and hungry for sound doctrine.

What does it all mean? This: Almost from the beginning of Christianity religious feeling has expressed itself in unmistakable accents among the mystics. From time to time these accents can be and are muffled: but it is impossible, in England any more than in the Low Countries, totally to destroy a religious impulse which has produced some of the most inspired pages in our national literatures. Moreover, interest in the writings of the medieval mystics is as clearly marked among some of the brethren separated from us by the Protestant Reformation as it is among Catholics; and that seems to be one of the most striking testimonies to the hidden working of divine grace—which is one and indivisible—in the body of the Church which is materially so grievously divided. These Protestants, devouring the works of Ruysbroeck or Thomas a Kempis but withholding themselves from the religious authority that those mystics obeyed, are in much the same case as John Henry Newman. In the days before his reconciliation with her, Newman had some very hard things to say about the Catholic Church; but all the time he loved her passionately without knowing it. Surely then reading the mystics can do nothing but good for those souls who seek to serve God in truth; and accordingly, when I was asked leave for the translation of these modest pages into English, it seemed to me I could not but agree.

Was it rash of me to write this book? Have I made an untimely essay in synthesis, falsifying the evidence by my undue haste? I do not think so. We have by now the components that are necessary for roughing-in the main lines of the development of spirituality in the Low Countries; these elements go back a long way, and the picture they make is becoming clearer every day. Time no doubt will show the need for slight modifications here and there; but if the Low-Countries mystics are studied against their background in history, I believe that they enable us to see what was personal in their religious experience, what they owed to their predecessors and what they handed on as a legacy to the generations that came after them. Only by connecting the links of the chain in a modest synthesis are we able to get an idea of the epic of the people of the Netherlands as they have sought God through the centuries.

STEPHANUS AXTERS, O.P.

# CHAPTER I

## Before Ruysbroeck

THE spiritual life of the Low Countries did not begin with Ruysbroeck, but long before that, no doubt at the time when the first attempts to spread the gospel of Christ were made there. But the present state of historical studies provides little information about Christian life in the early centuries of our history, and that whether we examine reliable sources or those that are far from reliable. We know that there were Christians in our lands before the barbarians arrived with fire and sword: there are two burial inscriptions[1] of the fifth century that are indisputable evidence of this. We know, too, that from the middle of the fourth century, or a little earlier, these Christians formed an organized Church with a bishop at its head. St Servais (Servatius) discharged this office from 346, or before, for St Athanasius mentions him in the *Apologia contra Arianos*,[2] among the two hundred and eighty-two bishops who upheld his cause. And that is about all we do know; for it would be very rash to try to add anything further by reference to the lives of those first apostles who seem to have preached the gospel from the Meuse to the North Sea. The *passiones* of St Quentin, of SS. Crispin and Crispinian, of St Piatus and St Lucian are riddled with legends, each one more improbable than the last, to such a degree that it can be said of these documents that in them the marvellous takes the place of the spiritual. But in any case this early phase of Christianity did not last long. With the beginning of the fifth century the barbarian hordes streamed over Gaul, sweeping away Roman civilization and with it the first cells of Christian life on Belgic

9

soil. The bishopric of Tongres-Maastricht alone survived to be a link between pre-invasion Christianity and that which was to come.

According to Mr van der Essen we are no better informed about the centuries immediately following the Frankish invasions. It is the opinion of this distinguished historian that for the hagiographers of the earlier middle ages the word *virtus* signified, not virtue, but miracle; and he therefore concludes that in medieval hagiographical writings the saint was a wonder-worker rather than a man of heroic virtue. In 1907 Mr van der Essen made a very careful study of the lives of the saints of the Merovingian epoch,[3] and there found less evidence in support of his thesis.[4] It is then in the first instance a question of the centuries following the Frankish invasions. Actually, if we study the twelve Merovingian "lives" which specialists agree have not been subsequently touched-up, it will be found that these texts most certainly know the word *virtus* with the meaning of *virtue*. Not only that, but *virtus=virtue* is used almost as often as *virtus=miracle*—the first sixteen times, the second twenty-five times[5]; and most of these dozen texts give a portrait of the saint concerned in terms of his virtues. Furthermore, several of these documents deliberately dwell on their subject's virtues, for example, the great compassion for prisoners of St Erminus[6] and the goodness to the needy of St Eloi (Eligius)[7]. It is then quite clear that during Merovingian times in the Low Countries, as elsewhere, holiness was in the first place a matter of virtue.

When speaking of spirituality the first virtues to be considered are those which concern the inner life most directly and are as it were its clearest and fullest expression. Now it is true that the Merovingian texts concerned with the inner life are but few. However, the *Vita Geretrudis*[8], written about 742, tells us that St Gertrude of Nivelles was *orationibus dedita*, "persevering in prayer"; the *Vita Ursmari*[9] says the same of St

Ursmar; and the *Vita Arnulfi*[10] gives us reason to believe that meditation was the form of prayer favoured by several of these saints. The book used by St Gertrude for meditation was the Bible itself, which she "knew by heart".

These things are unquestionably spiritual and can denote a pre-mystical state; but for several of these saints prayer was merging into contemplation; for example, St Eloi (d. 660), who concentrated on Christ's wounds. There is no need for surprise that one of the Merovingian saints, namely, St Gertrude, experienced the mystical marriage with our Lord. Nor are wanting the phenomena that often go with mystical states: St Aldegund (d. 684) wrote down an account of her visions, which can be identified in chapters 5–17 of her *vita*.[11] In the Low Countries, then, the appearance of hagiography was soon followed by autobiography; and, though the point is not certain, there are those who maintain that St Aldegund wrote, or dictated, her thirteen visions in the Frankish tongue.

There is a third kind of document which must be mentioned for the sake of completeness: in its original state it is older than either of the two already mentioned. There is extant a text of sermons of St Eloi[12]. But their interest for the history of spirituality is slight, for they do not rise above the level of very elementary catechetics. (The sixteen homilies attributed to St Eloi by Migne[13] are in fact no older than the beginning of the ninth century.)

The Merovingian age was then the childhood of spirituality in the Low Countries, but it was none the less important: the buds of Christian life were everywhere beginning to burst into flower. It was between 625 and 650 that the monasteries of Elnone, Sithiu, Stavelot-Malmedy, and St Peter's at Mount Blandin were founded, and other foundations soon followed; and it was about this time that began what has been called the age of saints. For some hundred years they were more numerous than ever after in the history of the Low Countries;

Father Gabriel Théry, O.P., and Mr Ferdinand Lot[14] estimate the number of *vitae* of Merovingian saints at three hundred: and of these, seventy-nine belonged strictly to that part of the Merovingian kingdom which corresponded to the later Low Countries.

Towards the year 750, however, things were changing. Princes helped to pay for their often useless wars by means of secularization of the monasteries, and this was not the only factor in the tale of monastic decay, which was still further aggravated by the Norman invasions. This state of affairs lasted till the beginning of the tenth century, when monastic reform was undertaken with great results. Its chief promoters were St Gerard of Brogne (d. 959), Bd Richard of Saint-Vanne (1046), and St Poppo of Stavelot (d. 1048). Their work was not a strict following of that of Cluny—St Gerard's, indeed, came first by some years—but from a certain point they were parallel movements. But religious writers did not wait for monastic reformers to show them the way. As trees are strengthened by the wind that beats on them, so the dawning spirituality of the Low Countries gained in power and depth during the stormy days. What strikes one most in studying the religious literature of the Carolingian age is its liturgical inspiration. Thus, early in the tenth century, Stephen of Liége (d. 920) instituted a feast of the Most Holy Trinity for his diocese and himself provided the whole of its office, which from a musical point of view was, we are told, something quite new. But we are here more interested by the text of this office, both for its own sake and because of its evidence that the solemnity of the Holy Trinity is of Liegeois origin. The fact of this devotion of the Low Countries towards the Holy Trinity is confirmed by Pope Alexander II in his reply that the feast in question was not in accordance with Roman tradition[15], and by the celebration of the feast with an octave in the Flemish provinces from the end of the twelfth century. In 1199 Giles the Fleming was a party to a case in the king of England's court, and the pleadings are dated "on the octave-day of the feast of the Most Holy Trinity"[16].

However, it is not so much liturgical texts strictly so called, drawn up in the Low Countries, however notable they may be, that show the liturgical origins of a great deal of their religious literature. The *Pigmenta* of St Anscar (d. 965) are even more instructive. In the *Vita Anscarii* St Rembert tells us that his master drew up for his own personal use a series of short prayers, which he called *Pigmenta* because they made the recitation of the psalms more delightful to him, "ut ei psalmi hac de causa dulcescerent"[17]. (Ducange gives several examples of *pigmentum*, meaning wine mixed with honey.) Clearly these prayers were at the same time of private and of liturgical inspiration, so it can be said that they marked the birth from the liturgy of a new literary species, that of "elevations". But St Anscar (who also wrote a book of visions, of which his biographer makes use) was not the sole begetter of this species: it appears to have been brought to the Low Countries by Alcuin (d. 804), author of *Officia per ferias*, and it would seem that when he drew up prayers which would give greater zest to the psalms he was following the example of St John Cassian (d. *c.* 433). Nevertheless St Anscar was apparently the first in the Low Countries to realize the interest and value of this procedure. According to Renier of Liége[18], he soon had an imitator in St Wolbodo, bishop of Liége (d. 1021), and it is a great pity that the texts of both Anscar and Wolbodo are lost; for the *Pigmenta* which Lappenberg[19] attributes to the first named cannot be genuine, since it does not agree with the summary given by Rembert of Torhout in the *Vita Anscarii*. A monk of Lobbes, Rathier of Verona (d. 974) went a step further when he composed four "elevations"[20], which were added as an appendix to the *De corpore et sanguine Domini* of Paschasius Radbertus. Rathier was a man of fiery spirit, very self-centred, a writer of distinction, tolerably ambitious, much exposed to the biting tongue of gossip; but when he addressed Almighty God, this difficult character spoke in accents that were hitherto unknown to that age. Long before him, St Augustine was a master of the "elevation"; but it was Rathier who revealed all its long-hidden resources to the Low Countries.

I said above that religious literature gained in depth during the tempest that raged in the Low Countries for over a hundred and fifty years: and this was so above all in doctrinal insight. Here again the influence of the liturgy was preponderant. At this time all religious life found its centre in the Divine Office, *Opus Dei*, and the monks of St Benedict were the "professionals" of the *Opus Dei*. Accordingly their studies were directed almost exclusively to those writings from which the most essential parts of the Divine Office were drawn, which, indeed, provided almost the whole of its contents. These sources were three— the Bible, the Fathers of the Church, and the lives of the saints. Some writers applied themselves to arranging scriptural texts in the ways calculated to be the most useful. Wazelin II (d. 1158), abbot of St Lawrence's at Liége, did this in a treatise called *De concordia Evangeliorum et expositione eorum*[21]; and Rudolph of Saint-Trond did the same thing, but using texts from the Fathers side by side with those from the Bible. (His work, *Liber sententiarum*, has not come down to us.) Others searched the patristic writings to find explanations of the more difficult parts of the Bible. Such an one was Alulfus of Tournai (d. 1140), who composed a biblical commentary with the help of passages drawn from the various works of St Gregory the Great.

But these monks did not stop there. They absorbed the very spirit of the Fathers, so that when we read some of the great Benedictine writers of the twelfth century we might well think we were in the age of St Gregory or St Ambrose. The reasoning is almost the same, and for the greater edification of the reader the literal sense of the Bible has often to give way to accommodated meanings. Franco of Afflighem (d. 1135), second abbot of the monastery at that place, is one of the most characteristic examples of Benedictine spirituality at that time. In his principal work, *De gratia Dei libri XII*[22], he argues as happily from Aaron's beard as from the grapes of the Promised Land. For him, dogmas of the faith are mysteries: he often calls them *sacramenta* and, like another Moses, takes off his shoes before approaching them.

The greatest of these Benedictine authors, and the most prolific of all the devout men in the Low Countries before Denis the Carthusian, is Rupert of Deutz (d. 1129), who ended his life as abbot of Deutz, near Cologne, after living over forty years at the abbey of St Lawrence at Liége. As soon as he was ordained priest, Rupert was appointed teacher in his monastery, and this appointment settled his career. As he says himself, he opened his mouth and thereafter never stopped teaching and writing. He never wearied of glorifying the mysteries of the Holy Trinity and the Redemption. The Christ whom he contemplated, and the love of whom he sought so earnestly to kindle in his readers, was not Christ suffering in human flesh but Christ in glory, triumphant over death. For him Mary was not the mother sharing the sufferings of her Son but rather, as Father Huijben has remarked, the prophetess at the foot of the cross.[23] To make this austere doctrine intelligible to his readers, Rupert abandoned the rudimentary exegesis of his elders, the juxtaposing of passages from the Fathers, and gave a coherent commentary on the sacred books. But he did not trouble much about the literal sense. In his commentaries on the Fourth Gospel, the Apocalypse, the Minor Prophets and elsewhere he allegorizes the inspired texts with remarkable skill, and he has no objection to interpreting the same verse of the Bible in several very different ways. He writes accordingly as his inspiration moves him, and indeed himself attributes his scriptural knowledge to his own visions and dreams. So it is easily understood that his utterances are not all equally happy. After reading the *De divinis officiis*, a liturgical *Summa* in which Rupert gives a symbolical explanation of the sacred offices, St Norbert (d. 1134) reproached him with teaching that the Holy Ghost took flesh in Mary's womb. It is however clear that the impugned passage is not inconsistent with the Church's traditional teaching[24]. But certain expressions in the same treatise[25] come close to teaching that after the consecration in the Eucharist the substances of Christ's body and of bread are, by a sort of hypostatic union, both present unchanged. Then his *De voluntate Dei liber unus*[26] got him into trouble with Anselm of Laon and William of Champeaux, and a theological battle followed, a contest which in certain respects was itself symbolical. Two methods of teaching were at grips: the old patristic method, which was the more in accord with the age-long traditions of the Benedictines, and the new dialectical method, the *fides quaerens intellectum* of St Anselm of Canterbury (d. 1109), who had a faithful Low Country follower in Bd Odo of Tournai (d. 1113). Rupert accused the upholders of the new method of lack of discretion in respect of Christian dogma. It should be loved, admired from a distance: but to go so far as to analyse it was like the disrespect of the younger son of Noah towards his father[27]. All Rupert's work was conceived in this spirit of filial piety and timorous wonder where dogma was concerned. He remains the most noteworthy and most attractive example of the austere, hieratic, spirituality that characterized the Benedictines of the eleventh and twelfth centuries.

The last years of the twelfth century saw a further change. Hitherto the spirituality of the Low Countries had been solemn and severe; now it began to be intimate, warm-hearted even. The influence of a new religious order was more and more taking the place of that of the black monks of St Benedict. The

first Cistercian foundation in the Low Countries was made at
Orval in 1132; others followed, so that the twelfth century can
be called that of the Cistercian monks, and the thirteenth that
of the Cistercian nuns. In the Low Countries, as in France, the
problem of love was at this time very much to the fore; and
before the end of the thirteenth century the anonymous author
of a life of our Lord in rime[28] lamented that poets now sang
only of war and love. It is difficult to accept the view of J.
Anglade[29], M. Anitchkof[30] and E. Wechsler[31] that the *poesie
courtoise* owed its preoccupation with love to the religious
mystics. Lacking proof of the contrary, it would seem that St
Bernard in his concern with the problem of love was as much
dependent on public opinion as were the profane poets. All the
factors that led these last to concern themselves with love to the
extent that they did are not certainly established. Many of
those who visited the Holy Places of Palestine during the
Crusades learned there a more intimate relationship with Jesus
Christ; and this doubtless counted for much. So did the
ever-increasing number of commentaries on the Canticle of
Canticles. But it would be more than rash to conclude from
St Bernard's independence of the profane poets that the twelfth
and thirteenth centuries' solution of the agonizing problem of
love owed nothing to him. On the contrary; in the Low
Countries, as elsewhere, it owed him much: it was due to him
that the spirituality of the end of the twelfth century and of the
hundred years that followed was concentrated around love. In
their newly-founded monasteries and in those affiliated to
Cîteaux, the Cistercians learned from him; the Canticle of
Canticles was their text-book. That is to say they saw our
Lord as the Bridegroom, above all, and related their mystical
experiences in the nuptial terms of the Canticle. Bernard of
Clairvaux was the example whom they followed. When he had
written that love of the crucified Jesus was his whole philosophy, Elias of Coxide (d. 1203) abbot of Les Dunes

embroidered the statement in one of his tender sermons[32], declaring that love of the crucified Jesus was all his logic, all his physics, all his ethics. Again, the threefold mystical kiss, on which St Bernard dwelt so often, inspired Gerard of Liége (who perhaps was abbot of Val-Saint-Lambert between 1249 and 1254) to a piece of writing on the same theme that is psychologically extremely penetrating. The work in which this appears, *Quinque incitamenta ad Deum amandum ardenter*[33], is a whole treatise on the love of God; and the *Septem remedia contra amorem illicitum*[34], though a much less notable work, can be regarded as a prelude to it. There must also be mentioned Gerard of Liége's treatise *De doctrina cordis*[35], which for centuries was wrongly attributed to the Dominican of the same name. It is a tiresome work to read because of the number of authorities cited, but until the end of the middle ages it was known over a wide area; its style is inferior to that of the *Quinque incitamenta*, but certain points in it are worth notice, for example, concerning the seven indications of ecstasy. Again, in the *Carmen de sancta cruce* of Arnold of Louvain (d. 1250), fifteenth abbot of Villers, we meet the lyrical outpouring after ecstasy; and the unpublished prayer to each of the members of the Crucified found in MS. 4459-70[36] of the Bibliothèque royale at Brussels is far better than that of St Bernard in Migne's *Patrologia latina*.[37]

Still confining ourselves to the Low Countries, there is more information available about the Cistercian nuns than about the monks of the same order; indeed their life during the thirteenth century provides one of the most moving chapters in the epic of the earlier Cistercians. During the Benedictine period of her life, St Lutgard of Tongres (d. 1246) experienced the "exchange of hearts", and she was the great lover of the Sacred Heart of her century. According to her biographer, she passed her days in closest intimacy with our Lord, his Mother and the saints; our Lady in particular is said to have appeared to her almost every day. Ida of Nivelles (d. 1231), referred to by the author of the *Vita Beatricis* as a woman of great worth, used to remind the nuns of La Ramée that when they bowed low at the *Gloria Patri* they were embracing the Most Holy Trinity. Beatrice of Nazareth (d. 1268) also had a very great devotion for this mystery, which was opened to her after Compline one day during the octave of Christmas; and her biographer relates that she always had some book about it close by her. Beatrice was also notably devoted to our Lady, and when she was still an oblate at Florival she already frequently used the Psalter of the Blessed Virgin, that is, the Hail Mary said one hundred and fifty times. From the documents at present available, it would seem that the origins of the rosary must be looked for in the Low Countries and the neighbouring German provinces. Except in the case of St Aybert (d. 1140)[38], a Benedictine of Crespin, near Valenciennes, practically all the documents bearing on the rosary in the thirteenth century are concerned with Cistercians or Dominicans.

There is no need to dwell on the thoroughly apostolic spirit of the nuns with whom we are concerned. St Lutgard undertook a seven-year fast because the Sorrowing Mother told her that the Albigensians were again crucifying her Son. Ida of Nivelles revealed their hidden offences to sinners, and her prayers for the souls in Purgatory seem to have been specially effective. Alice of Schaarbeek (d. 1250), a nun of the priory at La Cambre, was threatened with blindness due to leprosy, and offered the sight of her right eye to our Lord on behalf of the king of France, who was leading a crusade to Palestine. And these nuns, with many others, gave a fundamental importance to eucharistic piety. Thus, if we examine the origins of the *cultus* of the reserved Sacrament, we come upon the Cistercian, Bd Ida of Louvain (d. 1300). Then there is the vision of the new-born child in the Host which happened to her namesake of Nivelles one Christmas day—a good illustration of the desire to look at the Host which made itself felt in the Western church from the end of the twelfth century. Bd Juliana of Cornillon, who urged the institution of a feast in honour of the Blessed Sacrament upon the bishop of Liége, Robert of Torote, had more than one affinity with the Cistercians; and it was in fact Liége which gave us the festival of Corpus Christi—one of the most beautiful solemnities in the Church's worship.

The spirituality of a religious order cannot be understood without reference to the writings of its mystics, and the Cistercian nuns of the Low Countries had a writer of note in Beatrice of Nazareth. (She is so called because she died prioress of an abbey of that name.) She wrote an autobiography which was translated into Latin by William of Afflighem, when prior of the Benedictine monastery at Wavre (He was later abbot of Saint-Trond); but parts of it he only summarized, and in giving it a more didactic flavour he lost the personal touch of the original[39]. It should be noticed that the author of this *vita* uses the three-fold division of the interior life, making Book I correspond to the state of the beginner, Book II to the more advanced state, and Book III to the state of perfection; and it is not at all likely that he found this division in the vernacular text from which he was working. Nevertheless he was not the first in the Low Countries to make use of it, for the Dominican Thomas of Cantimpré (d. *c.* 1270) did so in the *Vita Lutgardis*[40]. This work was dedicated to the master general of the Friars Preachers, Humbert of Romans, and as his term of office lasted from 1254 to 1263 the *Vita Lutgardis* must have appeared during those years.

Except for one chapter, *Seven Ways or Degrees of Love*, the original text of Beatrice's work is lost, but the vernacular text of that chapter shows that William of Afflighem's Latin version is passably faithful.[41] Beatrice says nothing about the sort of love "which asks", which is love only in name, but begins straight away with the love "which asks not". The first step or state of love is the taking hold of the natural gifts, and what Beatrice meant by that appears in the chapter of her auto-biography *De eo quod ad cognitionem sui ipsius omnimodam aspiravit*. There she says that one day she realized that she had never valued natural gifts at their proper worth—such gifts as innate self-respect, intellectual discernment, inborn austerity, courtesy, inward peace. The second step is disinterestedness— the soul loves God simply for himself. The third is a toilsome state: the soul striving to serve God in an ever more perfect way, and continually disappointed by consciousness of her insufficiency. It is not till the fourth stage is reached that mystical experience, properly speaking, begins. Beatrice of course does not use this expression, but she emphasizes with pleasure that henceforward the soul remains passive in her commerce with God—she is indeed taken up, absorbed, con-sumed, engulfed, ravished by love. In the fifth state love rages in the soul, who feels torn and hurt thereby. The sixth step is when the soul, completely detached and mistress of her faculties, experiences true freedom. And finally, at the seventh step, the soul is consumed with longing: she lives more with the angels than on the earth, and looks only for liberation from the body that keeps her in this world.

The importance of this treatise for the history of spirituality in the Low Countries can hardly be exaggerated. When she dwells on the soul's natural endowments, innate self-respect, intellectual discernment and the rest, and the need for their development, Beatrice of Nazareth is preparing the way for that speculative mysticism some of whose finest achievements will soon appear both in Brabant and across the Rhine. It was in the *Seven Ways*, too, that the spirituality of the Low Countries seems first to have shown consciousness of "theo-pathic" states, for example, the soul's passivity during mystical experience; and, though the experts have so far been unable to date Beatrice's work within ten years, it is probable that the treatise was already written when Thomas of Cantimpré made his threefold division. Though she gave more importance to the function of the human understanding than did the first Cistercians, who simply wanted to be penitents, Beatrice retained the conception of love which she had received from her master, St Bernard: that is, her mysticism kept a definitely nuptial direction; she saw Jesus Christ as bridegroom, and longed with all her soul for the mystical marriage. But even during her lifetime this conception of love was giving way to another, and one quite new to the Low Countries.

The identification of the mystic called Hadewijch has been a nightmare to philologists for nearly a century. One of the latest hypotheses is that of Father J. van Mierlo, S.J., who seeks to identify her with a *béguine* of Nivelles named Helwig of Saint Cyr, who was buried at the abbey of Villers in 1269. However that may be, it seems to be established that Hadewijch was a *béguine*, and all her work suggests that she lived during the thirteenth century, probably about the middle. The writings of this person who is rather hard to identify include accounts of visions, letters, a number of strophic verses, and sixteen poems in *rimes plates*[42]. In them she takes her idea of love from the Cistercians, particularly from Beatrice of Nazareth, and gives it an unquestionably metaphysical sense.

The key to Hadewijch's spirituality is given in a phrase of one of her letters—"Love is all". For her the inner life consists wholly of an ascent, a great endeavour, towards love. Love is the attribute of God. God is love. And the personal character of love is such that the movement towards it becomes a duel between the soul and God, which is the theme of most of Hadewijch's poems. Everyone who looks into himself finds there a pronounced leaning towards God; and Hadewijch, faithful to St Augustine's introversion, calls this the need of the soul. It is because of it that, when the soul has become conscious of herself, the psychic threefold is moved to seek the divine Threefold; we are an image of the Trinity, and that image tries to come close to the Most Holy Trinity. But it will succeed only if it gets at the life which the soul leads in God from all eternity. So Hadewijch is really an exemplarist. She seems indeed to have been the first in the Low Countries to look at human existence from this angle, which at first sight is disconcerting for anybody not familiar with Neoplatonism. As Hadewijch sees it, we are not yet what we are; we have not "spotted" what is already ours; we are still far from that which appertains to us[43]. Allusion to a life which is other than that of every day occurs three times, and is well explained by another passage, in which she reminds a disciple that she must take into consideration the state of dignity in which in the beginning God loved and chose her[44]. This primeval dignity must not be identified with "original justice", which Hadewijch seems rather to have in mind in Letter VI. It is Hadewijch's pretty unambiguous exemplarism that gives efficacy to the longing of the ternary-image to come closer to its exemplary ternary-cause. The Father pours himself out upon us, sending us the Word; and the Word returns to the bosom of the Father. The Father pours himself out upon us, sending us the Holy Spirit; and calls the Spirit to return to him, together with all that the Spirit has inspired.

It may be noted that Hadewijch says nothing about the return to the bosom of the Father of all creatures comprehended in the Word, archetype of creation: she refers only to that other return which is grafted upon it, of the elect and of all meritorious works, together with the Holy Spirit who has inspired them. She prefers to look at our adherence to the Word according to the historical order of the Redemption rather than according to the ontological order. Our salvation depends on our devotion to Jesus Christ; but the distinction between devotion to his manhood and of devotion to his godhead is always something of an abstraction: in the concrete order they go together. Effective virtues, the humility, brotherly love, patience in adversity that are the essence of Christianity, are learnt in the school of Christ crucified; and this following of the crucified Lord is disinterested. The chosen of God do not serve Love for reward, not even for Heaven itself: their love for him is its own reward—Hadewijch sets this out several times, with arguments in the manner of the "courtly" poets. It is then daily exercise of virtue that prepares the soul for those divine "touches" with which mystical experience begins. We are made like to the Incarnate Word by suffering; and we can return to the bosom of the Father only when steeped in the image of the crucified Son.

These are only a few of the elements in an exceptionally rich body of doctrine. Hadewijch's spirituality is undeniably affective, and examination of it from this point of view can hardly fail to reveal more than one affinity with that of St Bernard. But her outstanding achievement is to have given a metaphysical basis to that spirituality which the Low Countries had received from the Cistercians: Hadewijch's work stamped Neoplatonic exemplarism with an authentic Christocentrism half a century before Rhenish exemplarism had appeared. Nor is that all. Hadewijch did what, in the opinion of Etienne Gilson[45], St Bernard did not do: she spiritualized courtly love. This was more than simply the use of a score of terms of gallantry, borrowed directly or indirectly from the *trouvères* of northern France; she took away its human direction from my Lady's service, so that courtly love could be transposed into a metaphysical key, and integrated this regenerated conception of love into a doctrine of mystical experience.

Nevertheless Hadewijch was far from having said the last word. Some years ago Father Reypens discovered, in a manuscript that is in a fair way to become famous, a Commentary on the Our Father[46], which is attributed to a certain Gerard Appelmans, of whom about the only thing known is that he was a hermit, living in a forest. This short commentary is far too slight to enable us to know the author's spirituality, but it clearly shows a Trinitarian exemplarism even more explicit than Hadewijch's. While she goes no further than the return to the Father's bosom of the Holy Spirit with all the good of which He has been the inspiration in the faithful, Appelmans refers also to a return of all that the Father has conceived; and more remarkable still, he connects the non-immanent emanation that constitutes creation with the immanent emanation of all created forms. His introversion, too, is yet more marked than Hadewijch's. The Father conceives the Word in the depth of our soul; but the soul can grasp what he is saying within her only if she listens to it spiritually. Finally, Appelmans devotes some particularly suggestive sentences to the apostolic aspect of mystical experience. Thanks to the merits of the mystics (a word which for him is synonymous with saints), we deserve to share in the merits of Christ's passion—Appelmans in a way makes the mystics our co-redeemers.

Thus, thanks to Beatrice of Nazareth, to Hadewijch, and to Gerard Appelmans, the main lines of mystical experience were sketched in the literature of the Low Countries by the end of the thirteenth century.

Early in the next century there were written two modest little Dominican works in which we seem to catch an echo of the more weighty expositions of Beatrice, of Hadewijch and of Gerard Appelmans. The first is a letter of advice from Henry of Louvain to a devout lay person. Friar Henry insists above all on inward quiet as an indispensable condition of religious experience; God can be reflected only in a soul that is completely submissive to his will. This letter was so widely known because in 1543 St Peter Canisius included it with other pieces in a collection of Tauler's sermons; by 1552 Surius had translated it into Latin, and henceforward it was found in most editions of Tauler.

The other writing is a sermon, delivered about 1324 by a lector of theology, Nicholas of Strasburg, at a Dominican chapter in Louvain. It is called the *Sermon on the Golden Hill*[47]; and it preaches unquestioning reliance on Christ's merits to such a degree that a disturbed soul one day asked John of Schoonhoven (d. 1432) what he thought about it. Whereupon Schoonhoven wrote a short *Declaratio*[48] defending the orthodoxy of the sermon: there is nothing but those merits, he declared, of which mankind can avail itself.

# REFERENCES

[1] Dr A. W. Byvanck, *Excerpta romana, de bronnen der romeinsche geschiedenis van Nederland*, vol. II, p. 75 (The Hague, 1931–5).

[2] *Patrologia Graeca*, vol. 25, cols. 336–7.

[3] *Étude critique et littéraire sur les Vitae des saints mérovingiens de l'ancienne Belgique*. (No. 17 of Recueil de travaux publiés par les membres des conférences d'Histoire et de Philologie, Université de Louvain, 1907).

[4] "Jean d'Ypres ou de Saint-Bertin, 1383", in *Revue Belge de Philologie et d'Histoire*, vol. I, p. 477 (1922).

[5] For further information see the present writer's article, *Over Virtus en Heiligheidscomplex onder de Merowingers* in *Miscellanea Historica in honorem Alberti de Meyer*. (No. 22–3 of the series III of Recueil de travaux publiés par les membres des conférences d'Histoire et de Philologie, Université de Louvain, 1946.)

[6] W. Levison, in *Mon. germ. hist.*, *Script. rer. mer.*, vol. VI, (1913), pp. 461–70.

[7] B. Krusch, in the same, vol. IV, (1902), pp. 663–741.

[8] B. Krusch, in the same, vol. II, (1888), pp. 456, 33–4.

[9] W. Levison, in the same, vol. VI, (1913), pp. 455, 14.

[10] B. Krusch, in the same, vol. II, (1888), pp. 441, 12–17.

[11] *Acta Sanctorum Belgii*, vol. IV, (1787), pp. 315–24.

[12] B. Krusch, in *Mon. Germ. hist.*, *Script. rer. mer.*, vol. IV, (1902), pp. 751–61.

[13] *Patrologia Latina*, vol. 87, col. 593–654.

[14] *Histoire générale*, ed. Glotz, vol. II, *Histoire du Moyen Age; La civilisation carolingienne, La vie intellectuelle* (Paris 1928) vol. I. p. 623.

[15] *Micrologus de ecclesiasticis observationibus*, cap. LX; in *Patrologia Latina*, vol. 151, col. 1020.

[16] Cf. A. Wauters, *Table chronologique des Chartes et diplômes imprimés concernant l'histoire de la Belgique* (Coll. Académie royale des sciences, des lettres et des beaux-arts de Belgique, Commission royale d'Histoire), Brussels, 1871; vol. III, p. 112.

[17] G. Waitz, in *Script. rer. Germ. in usum scholarum ex Monumentis Germaniae historicis recusi* (Hanover, 1884), p. 68.

[18] *Vita Wolbodonis*; in *Patrologia Latina*, vol. 204, col. 209.

[19] *Sti Anskarii Pigmenta*, in *Zeitschrift des Vereins für Hamburgische Geschichte*, vol. II, (1847), pp. 1–32.

[20] *Patrologia Latina*, vol. 146, col. 443–50.

[21] Manuscript no. 10751 in the Bibliothèque royale, Brussels.

[22] *Patrologia Latina*, vol. 166, col. 717–808.

[23] *Les origines de l'École flamande: l'École bénédictine*, in *La Vie Spirituelle*, vol. LX, (1939), p. 182.

[24] *De divinis officiis*, lib. III, cap. XI; in *Patrologia Latina*, vol. 170, col. 67.

[25] The same, *loc. cit.*, col. 35.

[26] *Patrologia Latina*, vol. 170, col. 437–8.

[27] *De divinis officiis*, prolog., *loc. cit.*, col. 11–12.

[28] *Vanden levene ons Heren*, ed. W. H. Beuken (Purmerend, 1929), p. 161.

[29] *Les Troubadours: leurs vies, leurs œuvres, leur influence* (Paris, 1908), p. 68.

[30] *Joachim de Flore et les milieux courtois* (Rome, 1931), p. 104.

[31] *Das Kulturproblem des Minnesangs: Studien zur Vorgeschichte der Renaissance* (Halle, 1909), vol. I, p. 306.

[32] *Patrologia Latina*, vol. 209, col. 991–1006.

[33] *Analecta Reginensia: Extraits des manuscrits latins de la reine Christine conservés au Vatican*, ed. A. Wilmart, O.S.B. ("Studi e Testi"; Vatican City, 1933), pp. 205–47.

[34] The same, pp. 183–205.

[35] *Liber de doctrina cordis*, Paris, 1506; f. 9. IV r; The Bodleian Library at Oxford has a copy of this edition.

[36] F. 150r–52r.

[37] Vol. 184, col. 1319–24.

[38] *Vita Ayberti*, in *Acta Sanctorum*. April, vol. I, p. 674.

[39] I have used the Brussels manuscript Bibliothèque royale, 4459–70, f. 66–138. The text of C. Henriquez in *Quinque prudentes virgines* (Antwerp, 1630, pp. 1–167) is somewhat incomplete.

[40] *Acta Sanctorum*, June, vol. IV, pp. 187–210.

[41] French trans. by J. Kerssemakers, "Une mystique des Pays-Bas . . . ", in *La vie spirituelle*, suppl., vol. XIX (1929), pp. (307–332).

[42] The reader must be referred to the editions by Father J. van Mierlo, S.J., between 1924 and 1948 (Leuvense Tekstuitgaven series, Louvain), except for the *Mengeldichten*, which he has not republished since 1912.

[43] *Brieven*, br. VII, 29–32.

[44] *Brieven*, br. XVIII, 7–10.

[45] *La théologie mystique de saint Bernard* (Paris, 1934), p. 215.

[46] *Gheraert Appelmans' Glose op het Vaderons*, ed. L. Reypens, S.J., in *Ons Geestelijk Erf.*, vol. I, pp. 81–107 (1927).

[47] *De preek op den gulden berg. . .* , ed. S. Axters, O.P., in *Tijdschrift voor Taal en Letteren*, vol. XXVIII, pp. 20–39 (1940).

[48] The same, pp. 40–1.

# CHAPTER II

## RUYSBROECK

HADEWIJCH'S mind worked intuitively, and her manner of writing was massive, even heavy: reading her, we breathe the air of romanesque church-building. Bd John van Ruysbroeck (Rusbrochius; d. 1381) took up the problems that she had hardly touched, and developed them in a style that is never wearisome and sometimes takes lyric flights—his atmosphere belongs to the gothic churches.

Hadewijch handed the thirteenth-century watchword on to Ruysbroeck; and like her he spread it far and wide, in two words that sum up a whole pattern for living: "Love Love"[1]. This Love whom we must love is God. Ruysbroeck's theodicy is well developed, and it is set out most fully in the *Book of the Twelve Beguines*. He calls God our superessence, the exemplary image, the principle and the eternal end of every created thing. In Ruysbroeck the concept of "nature" seems to prevail over that of "person", and he seeks to explain the trinity of persons in function of the unity of nature: that unity is nature's throne, her foundation. But we must not be misled by his interest in the unity of nature. While a neo-platonist would naturally be more stirred by the return into the One than by our issuing from Him, it is always a matter of our trinitarian affinities; from the first it is with the dogma of the Trinity that Ruysbroeck connects our existence and supernatural life.

Like Hadewijch, he attributes to us a life from all eternity in the Word; and—what Hadewijch did not do—he justifies it by putting a comma after *nihil* in verse 3 of the prologue to St John's Gospel and joining *quod factum est* to what follows, as subject: 'That which was made was life in Him'. So all creatures

29

are born eternally by the eternal generation of the Word, before having been created in time; and from eternity they are alive in God, for all that is in God is God. This life continues always in the Father; it flows along with the Word; and it comes back to the Father's bosom with the Holy Spirit. And so, by the ideal or pre-real life that we all live in God, Ruysbroeck makes us participate in some sort in the triune life. Nor is there anything surprising in that, for there is only a rational distinction* between God and our pre-real life. We can say then that we live eternally in our quality as images of the Holy Trinity and the paternal oneness.

Ruysbroeck explains our life in time by reference to our pre-real life. In *The Adornment of the Spiritual Marriage* he recalls that this pre-real life in God is the principle of our created being in time to such a degree that our created being is continuous with the eternal being and is but one with it in essential existence. Now as our pre-real life belongs to the very life of God, so our life in time is in his divine image; and thus Ruysbroeck arrives at the threefold structure of the soul. According to him there are by nature three unities in every man, in the sinner no less than in the righteous. The first and highest of these unities, on which all creatures depend in their essence, for their life and for their preservation, is in God. This unity does not sanctify us: we have it in ourselves, and at the same time above ourselves, and without it we should simply founder into nothingness.

The second natural unity is that of the higher powers, made one by the fact that their natural origin, from the point of view of their activity, is in the unity of the spirit. These higher powers are three, *viz.*, memory, understanding and will, and they show three characteristics: essential bareness appertains to the memory, speculative perspicuity to the understanding, and

---

* *Distinctio rationis* in the strict sense of a distinction which is not real but of the mind only.

the spark in the soul, her natural inclination towards her origin, to the will. These three properties constitute a single living ground and substance, the province of the higher faculties; and it is above all in virtue of these three properties that the soul is an image of the Holy Trinity: image of the Father through the imageless nudity in the memory, image of the Son through the speculative ability, or higher reason, in the understanding; image of the Holy Spirit through the spiritual spark in the will. And therefore the effects of these properties are attributed respectively to one or other of the persons of the Holy Trinity. Finally, the more the three faculties tend towards their common ground, towards the substance of the soul, the more the soul will be disposed to mystical experience—provided she does not puff herself up with the deceptions of false mysticism.

The third natural unity is the domain of the lower powers, which have their seat in the heart as principle and source of animal life, and all bodily and sensual activity springs from it. So the third unity makes man sensory and animal; the second makes him rational and spiritual; and the first keeps him in being. But it should be remarked that the second is not really distinct from the first: they differ only accordingly as and to the degree that the unity is looked at from its operative aspect or its essential aspect.

But these three unities do not exhaust the structure of the soul which, as conceived by Ruysbroeck, requires also an obediential power; but this he does not discuss, leaving it implicit in his writings. What then were his ideas about this power?

In the *Summa theologica* (Ia IIae, qu. 113, a. 10 c) St Thomas Aquinas answers the question: *Utrum iustificatio impii sit opus miraculosum?* by the assertion that the soul is by its very nature capable of receiving grace, because it is made in God's image. Ruysbroeck says the same in his *Mirror of Eternal Salvation.* But the question is whether this capacity is to be understood as absolute, that in the state of primitive righteous-ness nature and grace had been raised to the same level; or whether it is to be understood very relatively, nature simply having a predisposition to be raised to the plane whereon it can receive an inpouring of grace. Certain passages of Ruysbroeck give the impression that he recognized in grace only a healing function, nature being able of itself to reach the Beatific Vision, and this is how the Benedictines of Saint-Paul de Wisques understand him in *The Mirror of Eternal Salvation*. They interpret him as believing that 'the higher faculties are . . . faculties of the divine, made for its attainment, provided they are sufficiently disengaged from earthly things and so find no obstacle between them and the things of God. According to our author, the power of obedience for these faculties then consists in letting oneself be purified by God; and this necessary purification is the work of grace'[2]. A passage in the *Book of the Supreme Truth* seems to support this interpretation: it points to the conclusion that for Ruysbroeck the three unions, the most sublime no less than the humblest, are actual for every man here below; for he declares that these unions are no less in nature than in grace and glory[3]. But the following chapter shows clearly that, in writing the passage just referred to, Ruysbroeck was thinking of the righteous, the justified, and of no one else[4]. For if union by intermediary is for them alone, the same must be true of the other two unions, for they are higher in every way.

We look in vain for a second reference in Ruysbroeck's works to a natural union of the soul with God. And it would therefore seem that Waffelaert[5] understands the disputed passage more correctly when he says that, when the sentence about the three unions was written, Ruysbroeck was not considering grace, but at the same time did not wish to exclude it as irrelevant to the union in nature. Other passages support this interpretation. In the first of his works, *The Kingdom of the Lovers of God*[6], he makes a very clear distinction between creation and the gift of grace, in respect of angels as well as of men; the *Mirror of Eternal Salvation*[7] says that the vesture that is Christ's by nature is ours only by grace. Text could be opposed to text indefinitely; but it must be added that Waffelaert's interpretation, rather than that of the Benedictines of Saint-Paul de Wisques, agrees with Ruysbroeck's fierce campaign against the Beghards as seen in his writings. The Beghards were condemned by the Council of Vienne in 1311 for teaching that the soul has no need of the Light of Glory in order to see God face to face.

Ruysbroeck's psychology then is no less striking than his theodicy, and the same with his theology, which for him is above all the science of grace and what it does in us. God gives grace in the second unity, that of the higher powers, in order that man may live virtuously, for it is always given with a view to action. Here Ruysbroeck's teaching is not consistent. Sometimes he compares grace with a slip that is grafted on to a tree, so that it appears to be something coming from outside; at other times he speaks of it springing up within us in the second unity as from a source which has only to wait for the propitious moment for it to begin to flow. And he quotes the word of St Augustine that God is closer to us than we are to ourselves. But when he speaks of grace, Ruysbroeck does not always mean the same thing. God first gives man an exterior grace, one that touches him from without—it may be a trying experience or the words of a preacher or the good example of a neighbour. At other times this grace moves us from within, when we see our faults clearly or call to mind Christ's sufferings or are frightened at the thought of Hell. Such graces are prevenient and not meritorious, predisposing us to the reception of that grace by which we merit eternal life. God gives us light, and by means of that light we can make a willed and perfect response. Of these two elements charity is born, and charity in its turn gives birth to perfect sorrow for sin and purification of conscience. All this is simultaneous, in the sense that one of these elements cannot abide a moment without the others.

Along with the inpouring of sanctifying grace goes that of the theological and moral virtues and the gifts of the Holy Ghost—grace is to the virtues what the substance of the soul is to her faculties: the one requires the others. The three theological virtues adorn and enhance the higher powers of the soul; the moral virtues adorn and enhance the four lower powers which constitute one of the three natural unities. But Waffelaert asks[8] whether Ruysbroeck taught that the moral virtues, of which he treats à propos the loftiness of the super-natural order, are really distinct from the natural moral virtues (of which he writes at length), or whether these last are simply raised higher. Rather surprisingly, for Waffelaert has just re-marked[9] on a passage in the Book of the Spiritual Tabernacle which presents the theological virtues as the principle and origin of the moral virtues. Nevertheless the real distinction of the infused moral virtues from the natural virtues can be supported from other places in Ruysbroeck's writings. Else-where in the Book of the Spiritual Tabernacle[10] he makes one or several moral virtues emanate from each of the gifts. And in The Adornment of the Spiritual Marriage[11] he refers to two virtues of justice, one, which he calls a divine or theological virtue, born of charity and the other not an offspring of charity. But it is clear that here the divine virtue of justice means the infused moral virtue and the other one is the natural virtue. It is a pity that because of the difficulty of the terminology the Benedictines of Saint-Paul de Wisques let the part of the sentence about the first of these virtues fall out of sight.

Simultaneously with the theological and moral virtues the Holy Spirit is poured into the soul in a seven-fold living stream. Ruysbroeck understands these gifts of the Holy Ghost as super-natural senses which enable us to understand the promptings

of the Spirit, and accordingly they are of fundamental importance for the mystical life. Many theologians are of the opinion
that, so far as ordinary Christian life is concerned, the virtues
are enough for the doing of a supernatural act: it is enough to
mention Froget[12], Gardeil[13], Garrigou-Lagrange[14]. Ruysbroeck
did not think so at all. In the *Book of the Spiritual Tabernacle*[15]
he teaches that nothing, no deed, no virtue, can be meritorious
without the help of the gifts. We can therefore understand why
in his view the gifts are absolutely inseparable from the virtues
and the virtues from the gifts, so much so that, according to the
book just referred to[16], each gift begets several virtues. But here
again he is not consistent, for in *The Adornment of the Spiritual
Marriage*[17] all the virtues are born of the gift of wisdom. In
explanation of the gifts of the Holy Ghost being seven in
number, Ruysbroeck argues from the seven-branched candle-
stick before the ark of the covenant, the seven horns of the
Lamb, the seven planets, and even the seven locks of hair on
Samson's head.

In that moment when sanctifying grace, the theological and
moral virtues, and the gifts are conferred, the soul meets God
a first time. This is what Ruysbroeck calls the union by intermediary, which all the righteous experience and which remains
so long as the soul continues in the state of grace. Since grace
and the virtues are the intermediary, there is nothing subjective
about this union: both on God's side and on ours it is objective
and real, and continues in the state of glory. The soul knows
it since that first phase of the spiritual life which Ruysbroeck
likes to call "the active life".

When she has attained a certain degree of maturity, the soul
encounters God in another way, in union without intermediary,
that is, without the intermediary of grace. This of course does
not mean that grace is not needed: grace on the contrary is a
prerequisite, but it is not enough for this union, which is
realized in the Holy Spirit. To attain it the soul must be

recollected; the higher powers must flow back towards their common source and mingle together again in the unity of the spirit. For Ruysbroeck, turning inward is the road, and the only road, to mystical experience: at the ground of the higher powers the soul knows those divine "touches" with which the mystical life begins. So Beatrice of Nazareth had understood the matter a century before, and Ruysbroeck simply developed it. These "touches" are a divine movement which, by means of a brighter light and a fuller love, raise a more imperative need of union with God in the soul. Union without intermediary is therefore a state of delight in which the soul rests, over and above the gifts, not active but set in the domain of essence and hidden from any intellectual act on our part. Ruysbroeck makes use of a comparison to illustrate this union: on a summer's day the atmosphere is so penetrated by the light and warmth of the sun that they cannot be separated; nevertheless each keeps its proper nature—air does not become light, or light air. But he does not find this comparison close enough, so he essays another—white-hot iron, in which the iron is not turned into fire nor vice-versa. So also is God present in the substance of the soul without becoming that substance, and when the higher powers come together in active love then the soul's union with God is realized without intermediary. It is hardly necessary to recall that Ruysbroeck assigns this second union to that second phase of the spiritual life which he calls "the interior life". Finally, Waffelaert[18] interprets it as a personal union of the soul with the Holy Spirit, and it would seem that no further explanation is required.

There are certain privileged souls who meet God in a third way, the way which Ruysbroeck calls, for want of a more suitable term, union without difference or diversity. These souls are those who have entered upon the last stage of the spiritual life, the unitive way, for which Ruysbroeck reserves the name of "the contemplative life". Here an unshakable faith is needed: the soul is motionless, bereft of all images, intent upon Him who, when the moment is come, will wholly possess her. According to several authorities on Ruysbroeck's teaching, this third union is characterized by a direct, but transitory, vision of God. It is Auger's opinion[19] that the difference, as conceived by Ruysbroeck, between this earthly contemplation of God and the beatific vision is solely the difference—great enough, indeed—between the conditions of life of mortals in this world and of the blessed in Heaven. Nobody is likely to question this; but it is surprising that Auger should then go on to say that Ruysbroeck believed the act of beatific vision to be possible in this life. Moller[20] is of the same opinion: he does not pursue the matter very far, but he considers the difference between the two visions to be only one of degree. The texts advanced in support of this view are nearly always those in Book III of the *Adornment of the Spiritual Marriage*; for instance, where Ruysbroeck writes that, 'Contemplatives are transformed by the action of the light that is born within them; they become one with that light, by which they are enabled to see and which they contemplate'[21].

The *lumen gloriae*, light of glory, seems to be absolutely necessary for the realization of this intuition of God's essence during earthly life; but, aware of the difficulties involved in such an explanation, Father Reypens emphasizes that the direct vision here below must be understood as a supplementary activity of the *lumen gloriae*[22]. Various authors lay stress on the transitoriness of this vision and Waffelaert goes so far as to call it an irruption, an *illapsus*, of God into the soul[23].

But this does not clear the matter up. In book III of the *Adornment of the Spiritual Marriage*[24] Ruysbroeck remarks that contemplatives are less apt to receive the divine splendour on earth than in Heaven; and indeed he says (in *The Sparkling Stone*) that there is a great difference between the glory of the blessed and the highest that can be attained in this life.

Chapter XI of the last-mentioned book, which is apparently very clear, has been used by Father Huijben[25] to refute the accepted exegesis of other passages which seem much less clear. It is true that the chapter cited gives little enough support to the thesis that is so dear to some of the best of Ruysbroeck's expositors; but it may well be questioned whether this is enough to demonstrate an interpretation of book III of the *Adornment of the Spiritual Marriage* which the text of that book does very little to justify. And there is yet more to this controversy. For instance, it may be asked whether the "inferiority" of the earthly vision of God can properly be explained simply by the degree of light from the divine essence, seeing that that essence is as much the object of the intuition of contemplatives in this world as it is of the vision of the blessed in the next. Or again, it may be asked whether it be not rash to argue from the course of our eternal life with the Word, and from his return into the Father's bosom, to an intuition of the divine essence. The theory of an immediate vision presents a problem in the intentional order, and it ought to be decided whether this problem should be settled in function of an ontological problem like that of the divine emanations; or whether knowledge through "co-naturality", which union in love implies, provides a quite sufficient explanation of the mystical experience. We contribute these reflections to the discussion, and leave it there.

As we have dealt with it so far Ruysbroeck's spirituality seems to keep to the two lives with which he is continually concerned, the eternal or pre-real and the created. But, considered separately, neither one of these lives is more comprehensible than the other, and accordingly we find Ruysbroeck sometimes talking of a third, which he calls the "living life". (It is a pity that in their translation the Benedictines of Saint-Paul de Wisques dropped this expression and substituted for it "higher life")[26]. This third life is not more our pre-real life in

God than it is our created life in time, but is our original relation to God, that is, the bond which joins our created life to our uncreated or eternal life. It does not remain inactive: rather is it continually renewing itself in new meetings between God and the soul. Nor is that all. Above this exercise of love there is the eternal fruition in which the union of the soul and God becomes in some sense a unity: all doing is God's, while the soul rests in a state of blessed stillness. When with the help of grace the soul discards all images and reaches this quiet with God in the abyss of love, then she enters into superessential beatitude—so called by Ruysbroeck because the soul has through fruition overpassed herself into God's essence. We may well understand that Ruysbroeck looked on this as the highest state which the human soul can know in this world.

More than one element in Ruysbroeck's spirituality is reminiscent of Hadewijch, as may be seen in our summary. But to problems that she scarcely nibbled at he gave an amplitude that the thirteenth century never thought of. Like her, he set out to give a metaphysical basis to mystical experience. We must not be taken in by the title of, or by the verse from the Bible that served as a skeleton for, the *Adornment of the Spiritual Marriage*: in spite of the seemingly nuptial "get-up" of his finest work, Ruysbroeck's spirituality was far nearer to that of St Augustine than to that of St Bernard. Like Augustine, he delved into the problem of love until he reached the metaphysical foundations of all supernatural love, the inner life of God, One and Triune. Ruysbroeck was less penetrating than Augustine but he had a much finer "architectural" sense—he belongs to the era of the great theological *Summae*. Under his hand Hadewijch's intuitions of genius grew into a synthesis, a construction of which it is difficult to decide which is the more impressive, its unity as a whole or the harmony and proportion of its parts. Again we must not be deceived. This great constructive power was not the whole of Ruysbroeck. His soul overflowed with tenderness in reflection on the wonders of man's redemption. It was precisely his religious experience, of which the hidden things troubled his philosophical spirit, that made him bring forth that solidly-built philosophy of theopathic states which we have been studying.

# REFERENCES

[1] Cf. *The Severn Steps of the Ladder of Spiritual Love*, trans. by F. Sherwood Taylor (1943), ch. 14.

[2] 'Les facultés supérieures sont des facultés du divin, elles sont faites pour le saisir, pourvu que, suffisamment dégagées des choses terrestres, elles ne trouvent plus d'obstacles qui les séparent des choses de Dieu. La puissance obédientielle, d'après notre auteur, consistera dès lors, pour ces facultés, à se laisser purifier par Dieu, et cette purification indispensable est l'œuvre de la grâce. . .', *Œuvres de Ruysbroeck l'Admirable*, trans. by the Benedictines of Saint-Paul de Wisques (Brussels, 1912–38), t. II, pp. 15–16.

[3] 'Behold, I have said this: that the contemplative lover of God is united with God through means, and also without means, and thirdly, without difference or distinction; and this I find in nature and in grace, and also in glory', *John of Ruysbroeck: The Adornment of the Spiritual Marriage, The Sparkling Stone, The Book of Supreme Truth*, trans. by C. A. Wynschenk Dom, ed. by Evelyn Underhill (New York, 1916), pp. 226–7. A new trans. of *The Adornment of the Spiritual Marriage* has been made by Eric Colledge and published in London in 1952 under the title *The Spiritual Espousals*.

[4] 'I will say that all good men are united with God through means. These means are the grace of God, and the sacraments of Holy Church, and the divine virtues, faith, hope and charity, and a virtuous life according to the commandments of God', Wynschenk Dom, *op. cit.*, p. 227.

[5] Waffelaert puts it thus: 'Nequaquam intelligenda est illa triplex unio in natura, excludendo vel objective praescindendo a gratia, sed solummodo abstrahendo formaliter a gratia, et ita ut referatur natura suo modo, nempe potentialiter, ad gratiam,

sicuti gratia quoque, ast modo diverso, refertur ad gloriam',
*Notanda quaedam utilissima in ordine ad rite intelligenda opera
scriptorum contemplativorum atque ipsam contemplationem
divinam exercendam* in *Collationes Brugenses*, t. XVII, 1912,
p. 421.

[6] Cf. *The Kingdom of the Lovers of God, now translated for
the first time from the Latin of Laurence Surius, the Carthusian,
together with an introduction by T. Arnold Hyde* (London-New
York, 1919), p. 4.

[7] No English translation of this work exists; so we
refer to *Jan van Ruusbroec, Werken, naar het standaard-hand-
schrift van Groenendaal uitgegeven door het Ruusbroec-
Genootschap te Antwerpen* (Malines-Amsterdam, 1934), t. III,
p. 169.

[8] Above, n° 5, p. 312.

[9] Above, n° 5, p. 311.

[10] Cf. *Jan van Ruusbroec, Werken*, . . . t. II, p. 131.

[11] Cf. *John of Ruysbroeck: The Adornment of the Spiritual
Marriage* . . ., p. 42.

[12] *De l'habitation du Saint-Esprit dans les âmes justes d'après
la doctrine de saint Thomas d'Aquin*, in the *Revue Thomiste*,
t. IV, 1898, pp. 150-1. Republished under the same title by
Lethielleux (Paris, 1900; p. 423).

[13] *La structure de l'âme et l'expérience mystique* (Paris, 1927),
t. II, p. 165.

[14] *Perfection chrétienne et contemplation selon saint Thomas
d'Aquin et saint Jean de la Croix* (Saint-Maximin, 1923), t. I,
p. 349.

[15] Cf. *Jan van Ruusbroec, Werken* . . . , t. II, p. 116.

[16] Cf. *Jan van Ruusbroec, Werken* . . . , t. II. p. 131.

[17] Cf. *John of Ruysbroeck: The Adornment of the Spiritual
Marriage* . . . , p. 151.

[18] Above, n° 5, pp. 434-5.

[19] *De doctrina et meritis Joannis van Ruysbroeck* (Louvain,
1892), pp. 136-7.

[20] *Alle de Werken van Jan van Ruusbroec de Wonderbare*, in
*nieuwere taal overgezet* (Bussum, 1912), t. I, p. 128d.

[21] 'By means of this inborn light they are transformed, and
made one with that same light through which they see and
which they see', *John of Ruysbroeck: The Adornment of the
Spiritual Marriage* . . . , p. 174.

[22] *Le sommet de la contemplation mystique chez le b. Jean de*

D

*Ruusbroec*, in *Revue d'Ascétique et de Mystique*, t. III, 1922, p. 269.

[23] Above, n° 5, pp. 493–4.

[24] Above, n° 3, p. 175.

[25] *Ruysbroeck et saint Jean de la Croix*, in *Études Carmélitaines*, t. II (1932), pp. 239–47.

[26] *Œuvres de Ruysbroeck l'Admirable*, Wisques edn., t. I, pp. 150–8.

# CHAPTER III

## "SPECULATIVE" SPIRITUALITY
### AFTER RUYSBROECK

SOME years ago Father Huijben presented Bd John Ruysbroeck as a solitary peak. After what has been said above,
any reader who may have questioned his greatness will surely
be ready to admit that Ruysbroeck was not only a peak, but
also the most impressive one in the religious literature of the
Low Countries. But whether he was so solitary as historians of
spiritual trends have been inclined to think is another matter,
and one which we will now proceed to examine.

We have seen that a little before Ruysbroeck's death the
strongly-flowing river of Netherlands religious writing divided
into two streams: one was a speculative spirituality, greatly
interested in mystical experience, and the other was more
practical, chiefly concerned with the problems of ascetical life.
At the origin of these diverse streams we find two religious of
Groenendael, respectively the cook, John van Leeuwen
(d. 1374), who entered the way of mysticism, and John van
Schoonhoven (d. 1432), master of arts of the University of
Paris, who undertook a more practical and more modest
asceticism. Both currents seem to have owed a lot to Ruysbroeck (we are too inclined to concentrate exclusively on the
bolder parts of his writings, wherein he examines the problems
of mystical experience), and they were closely connected with
one another at more points than one. Those masters of
spirituality who had a more practical turn praised Ruysbroeck
very highly. After his first two sermons to the community of
Windesheim John van Schoonhoven ceased to concern himself

with mystical experience, but in 1408 he took up the defence of Ruysbroeck's orthodoxy against Gerson's attacks ; and his reply[1] thereto showed him to be familiar with the most subtle distinctions. Again, Gerard Groote, founder of the Brethren of the Common Life, wrote to the canons of Groenendael*suggesting they should modify certain expressions in *The Adornment of the Spiritual Marriage* and offering his help in so delicate an undertaking. He was afraid that these expressions might hurt the reputation of their writer, whose thought he, Groote, valued so highly, 'sensum tamen patris habeo'[2]. On the other side, such a follower of speculative spirituality as Denis van Rijkel did not hesitate to stretch out the hand of fellowship to the leaders of *Devotio moderna*.

The first of Ruysbroeck's disciples in order of date was John van Leeuwen, who was the second recruit at the hermitage after Ruysbroeck, with his uncle John Hinckaert and Canon Franco van Coudenberg, had withdrawn from Brussels to Groenendael in 1343. From the first he was put in charge of the monastery kitchen, and he was engaged in this and other like employments almost till the end of his life. In spite of these duties, and in spite of the fact that he had never (as he declared in his *Book of the Magi*) been to school—other than that of St Peter and St Andrew, that is, the school of the Holy Spirit— John van Leeuwen found time to write a score of spiritual works. They are more weighty than varied, some of them deserve more consideration than others, and their total volume exceeds the output of Ruysbroeck himself, whose threefold division into a moral, a spiritual and a divine life they follow. John van Leeuwen sees the interior life as a circle, its second phase involving the first, and the third involving its two predecessors; but when it comes to examining each phase in

---

* The monastery of canons regular, in Brabant, founded by Franco van Coudenberg, John Hinckaert and John Ruysbroeck in 1343. *Translator's note.*

particular it is found that he understands the first in a much more negative way than does his master. With Ruysbroeck, the soul who has not yet got beyond this first phase (what he calls the active life) is engaged in the practice of the moral virtues, but according to John van Leeuwen should be concerned above all with rooting out every tendency to sin. They are agreed that the second phase shows a very clear and definite centring on Christ. In *The Mirror of Eternal Salvation* Ruysbroeck calls this phase the state of giving oneself up to the divine will in and through Christ; our Lord's life is the second of the three books from which every religious should choose his evening reading, and in it we find the pattern for ourselves. John van Leeuwen then is obviously under Ruysbroeck's influence when he urges us to hide ourselves in Christ's wounds, to take up our abode there where—and nowhere else—we shall see God. And for both writers the third phase is that of participation in the life of God, John van Leeuwen calling this phase "divine life", where the human soul is passive. It is to this spiritual height that love must attain, and the emphasis is upon love, for that alone can reach it—reason has no place there. It is not clear whether he means that all knowledge is henceforth useless, or whether—for want of a suitable term to designate a knowledge so completely different from discursive knowledge—he calls this new knowledge of God "love" because love will one day possess God as he is.

The mystical experience that characterizes this third phase is experienced in the depths of the soul, who contemplates God above all the images hitherto used. Does this mean a direct, immediate vision of the divine essence wherein, all created "kind" being insufficient, the divine essence "informs" the human understanding? Father Dorresteijn[3] is of the opinion that the treatise *Concerning What is Needful to be Poor in Spirit* gives little support to any such interpretation. On the other hand several passages in John van Leeuwen's writings deal with a vision face to face (they have been pointed out to the interested by Father Reypens[4]). It would, however, seem that John van Leeuwen was very little concerned with the theory of *species impressa*, and one may believe that the two interpretations read more into his words than the author meant, the one in view of the traditional explanation of Ruysbroeck's teaching, the other in view of the thomist thesis on knowledge.

Unless too much weight be given to a number of details, it may then be said that John van Leeuwen's whole spirituality can be found in conclusions drawn from Ruysbroeck; but he was a "man of the people", moreover one with a character of his own, and this gives a distinguishing flavour to his thought: for example, there is something very childlike in his devotion to the saints. He attributed his perseverance in the life of virtue particularly to the inspiration of St Paul and St Martin: to the first because he joined the contemplation of Mary Magdalen with the activity of Martha, to the second because he shared his cloak with a beggar. The only one among his contemporaries whom he praises is Ruysbroeck (who was his spiritual director); and he makes it clear that he regarded him more highly than any holy man of his time. Nor was he any more tentative in his judgements of writers. He had great respect for St Augustine's wisdom, and recurs to Hadewijch as to a very holy woman whose writings were more instructive than any others of her day; but when he turns his attention to Master Eckhart he loses all moderation. In his work *Against the Errors of Eckhart*[5] he treats him as a formal heretic, a conceited, headstrong, foolish man who had no more intelligence than a turnip. When reproved for such intemperate language, John van Leeuwen answered that a man should not be accused of indiscretion when he took on himself to refute a teacher who put forward views contrary to the mind of most theologians; if Balaam's ass, an irrational beast, could utter prophecy, he, Brother John, who at least was endowed with reason, had the right to speak; and moreover, he said, he had always distinguished between his opponent's mistakes and his human dignity. He was sure that in due time and place, Eckhart had asked for God's forgiveness; and were he to see his soul going up and down in Hell on a burning log he, John, would be ready to take his place to ransom him.

The three dated works of John van Leeuwen are spread over the years 1355–58, namely, the treatises on the *Five Kinds of Brotherly Love*, on the *Seven Signs of the Zodiac*, and the first on the *Ten Commandments of God*[6]. The last of these three texts, of which the author himself gives the dates (he refers also to several other of his works without dating them), appeared in the year before Ruysbroeck's *Mirror of Eternal Salvation*, which means that all John van Leeuwen's writings must have been composed more or less under the watchful eye of his religious superior.

Except for John van Schoonhoven—and he began to write only several years after Ruysbroeck's death—this was not so with Ruysbroeck's other disciples: they all belonged to other *milieux* than Groenendael, and so were subjected to other influences besides that of Ruysbroeck, notably that of the spiritual heritage of their respective orders.

The first of these religious orders in the Low Countries to show a dependence on Ruysbroeck was the Carthusians: it was during his lifetime that Gerard de Hérinnes drew up his *Prologue* to a collection of five of Ruysbroeck's works, and more recent scholars identify its author with the Carthusian Gerard de Sainctes (d. 1377). This *Prologue* must be dated between 1360 and 1370, and it is of interest to us on more than one count. It was this Gerard who, by particularly effective strokes of his pen, drew Ruysbroeck's character for posterity; a very engaging character it is too, and we get no idea of it from John van Leeuwen's panegyrics. It was Gerard also who first set out to expound Ruysbroeck's theory of the three unions.

He tells us that it was for lack of a more appropriate term that, having discussed union through intermediary and union without intermediary, Ruysbroeck called the third union, union without difference. According to Gerard, he would remedy any exaggeration implied in this term by a reminder that he meant by it no more than the union that our Lord asked for his disciples in his sacerdotal prayer. We owe this first explanation of some of Ruysbroeck's most difficult pages to the first Carthusian writer in the Low Countries.

But unquestionably the most important and most prolific of Low-Country mystical writers was Denis van Leeuwen, better known from his place of origin as Denis van Rijkel, and better still in English-speaking countries as Denis the Carthusian (d. 1471): in the Montreuil-sur-Mer edition his works run to forty-five quarto volumes[7]. His writing began with a rather characteristic work, *De ente et essentia*, of which the text is lost as he later judged it desirable to modify it as he found it too thomist. Denis's interest in philosophy progressively lessened the older he got, but he always remained the most scholastic of the Low-Country mystics.

It was in his *De fonte lucis ac semitis vitae* that Denis established three stages that must be gone through by all who aspire to perfection—the purgative, illuminative and unitive ways. The first of these, he says, is a time of struggle with the numerous dire consequences of sin; it calls for exercise of the moral virtues, and the gifts which the soul specially needs are piety, knowledge, fortitude and the fear of the Lord. Meditation is the form of prayer best adapted to this phase of the spiritual life, and it is itself laborious prayer, being as it were a contest with the theme that has been chosen. The themes most recommended are God, the earthly life of our Saviour, and the four last things. The purgative way is the " way of the good servant".

The illuminative way on the other hand is a way of

contemplation of the sublime mysteries of our faith, particularly the hidden life of God, the Most Holy Trinity, and the special graces that we receive. For this, the soul's chief needs are the intellectual virtues of prudence, art, wisdom, knowledge and judgement, fortified by the gifts of counsel and understanding. The form of prayer proper to this way is a rather undeveloped contemplation, that is, contemplation by way of affirmation, of which contemplation by way of causality and by way of eminence are simply two variants: this sort of contemplation must not be confused with that of the philosophers. This second way is the " way of close friends".

The third, unitive, way is entirely a state of love, and accordingly the theological virtues, faith, hope, charity, are necessary above all since they set the soul's attitude towards God; to them must be joined the Holy Spirit's gift of wisdom. The soul is now further advanced in contemplation, and is in that negative way, or " by elimination", which Denis by choice calls mystical theology. In the earlier stages the soul saw eminently in God all the good she had found in his creation: now she disregards that, as totally inadequate to express the divine perfections, and seeks to contemplate God in the " cloud of unknowing". Such contemplation by elimination is far more perfect than that which went before, and, as a good scholastic, Denis raises the question whether it is an act of the understanding or of the will. His answer is that it cannot be an act of the will, because it is identical with that wisdom which has its seat in the understanding. Nevertheless, the act of contemplation by elimination has certain effects in the affective sphere; and so this "mystical theology", essentially an act of the understanding, is also connected with the heights of the will, in certain complementary aspects, *quoad complementum*, and by that in it which naturally urges it in that direction[8]. Finally, the unitive way is the way of "well-beloved sons and daughters".

Ruysbroeck's writings have a special place in the vast learning of Denis the Carthusian. He pauses at pre-real existence,
at union without intermediary, at the surge of the faculties
towards the soul's depths, at the "spark" in the soul, and at
other ideas which at once make us think of Ruysbroeck. And
we begin to wonder whether Denis believes that his mystical
theology, contemplation by elimination, must lead to direct
vision of the divine essence in this life, albeit a passing vision;
or at the very least that it may do so, without derogating from
the laws that govern our life on this earth. At first sight he
does seem to think so. He allows such direct sight to Moses
and to St Paul, and adds that after those precedents it would
be rash to deny it to our Lady. But if Moses, St Paul and our
Lady were so privileged, it still might be simply by way of
miracle—and in that order of things the possibilities are un-
ending. Where the ordinary run of Christians is concerned,
Denis admits his complete incompetence to judge. When he
is explaining the pertinent passages of Ruysbroeck, however,
he cannot avoid the issue; and he then explains the vision of
God here below as Ruysbroeck understands it in the Dionysian
sense of contemplation by negation[9].

But this question of how far direct vision of the divine
essence in this life is in accord with the principles of Denis's
spirituality must be insisted on, for contemporary studies in
mystical theology give it a very special interest. And it seems
that the answer can be found only in Denis's teaching about
beatitude. He distinguishes two beatitudes, one natural, the
other supernatural, and both consist in knowledge of God.
But natural beatitude is not the same for every intellectual
being: for God, it consists in the immediate vision of his own
essence; for angels, in knowledge of God by help of a *species
impressa*; for humankind, in knowledge of God by the way of
causality. So it is clear that Denis's doctrine of natural beatitude does not help us to solve our problem. But he also

distinguishes four supernatural ways of knowing God, of which the fourth alone concerns us at the moment. They are faith, contemplation, appearings and direct vision, and it is in this last way that the blessed know God. All created kind being insufficient of itself to express God's essence, only an un-created "kind" can do so; and therefore God's essence acts as "kind", as known object and formal reason. This formal reason, the exalted light of the divine essence—the *lumen gloriae*, in fact—is given to the blessed in an habitual manner (God could of course withdraw it if it seemed good to him so to do). But is it also given to devout Christians while still in this world? Denis says not, so far as the normal economy, the *lex communis*, of the spiritual life is concerned; and he is quite unequivocal about this (see *In libros Sti Dionysii Areopagitae: de Mystica Theologia*, cap. I, art. 4). The examples of Moses, of our Lady and of St Paul are then something outside this common law, miracles; and it therefore would seem that the possibility of intuition of the divine essence in this life is not in line with Denis the Carthusian's theology.

But the Carthusians were not the only religious among whom Ruysbroeck's teaching made headway. There were the Friars Minor, whose initial orientation as received from their founder was so different from that of Ruysbroeck. It is clear that the Franciscan Henry Herp (d. 1477) belonged as a writer to the school of speculative spirituality; and it can be assumed that this bent of mind was one of the reasons why he left the Brethren of the Common Life in 1450 to become a Friar Minor of the strict observance. In the dedication of the Latin edition of Ruysbroeck that was published at Cologne in 1609, Gerard Kalckbrenner, a Carthusian, wrote that all that was best in books II and III of Herp's *Mystica Theologia* was due to Ruysbroeck; and it is not without reason that others have said the same thing. One has only to consider Herp's threefold division of the interior life into active, spiritual and superessential;

his exemplarism, the introversion prerequisite to mystical experience; and the trinitarian orientation of his union of the soul with God. On the other hand, Herp prefaces his account of the superessential life with several very personal pages on the twelve mortifications; he did not get his chapter on the nine degrees of renunciation from Ruysbroeck; and his theory of aspirations, repeated acts of faith and love which he makes the nerve-centre of the interior life, is all his own.

The question whether he depends on Ruysbroeck in the matter of a direct vision in this life is more difficult. Ruysbroeck taught that intuition of the divine essence is a fact among those mystics who attain union without difference; and we naturally ask whether this intuition is an exceptional grace, off the beaten track of the mystical life, or whether it is the normal end to which mystical life must attain here below if it is to reach its full fruition. On this point Ruysbroeck never enlarged— whether because he thought the question idle we do not know. But Herp was quite forthright about it. Without any beating about the bush he said that intuition of the divine essence, vision face-to-face, is given to some contemplatives in this life; in explanation, he appealed to the *lumen gloriae*, earthly direct vision being as it were an anticipated and transitory glory.

Herp, then, was from afar the closest follower among Ruysbroeck's disciples; but for that very reason his *Eden contemplativorum* and *Mirror of Perfection* (a popular recasting of the first of these books) are better illustrations of the development of spirituality in the Low Countries than are the works of several other writers. Father Lucidius Verschueren[10] remarks that Herp's tone is not that of his master, in spite of the fact that he so often takes up the same arguments as Ruysbroeck, sometimes almost in the same words. Herp is more affective and does not stop short of practical application, while maintaining the philosophical bases of the unitive life as Ruysbroeck understood them.  Furthermore, in the matter of style and presentation, he adopted a more didactic, and therefore quieter, phraseology instead of Ruysbroeck's poetic lyricism. That Herp was not always an echo of his master is shown also by the reaction to his work. Ruysbroeck never got into trouble with the authorities; but the writings of the Franciscan (who was guardian of their friary at Malines) were taken unfavourable notice of no less than four times. On the last occasion all editions which did not conform with the text of the Roman edition of 1585 were put on the Tridentine index of forbidden books. In France St Francis de Sales, after encouraging Madame Brûlart to read the *Gospel Pearl*, warned the Philothea of the *Introduction à la Vie Dévote* against the dangers of seeking the supereminent life for herself; this was simply Herp's superessential life, whose name had been altered in the French translation of 1605.

Herp's influence was considerable. Several of the works of Francis Vervoort (d. 1555), another Friar Minor, for instance *The Wilderness of the Lord*[11] and *De Pane angelorum*[12], are unbroken aspirations towards the Well-Beloved; but it is particularly in his *Wedding Garment of God's Love*[13] that we see Ruysbroeck's teaching through the mind of Henry Herp. When Vervoort says that the soul, before entering a theopathic state, leans towards the Father, we hear an echo of Ruysbroeck's return of all created things to the Father's bosom. In the matter of grace Vervoort is much more explicit. He never mentions Ruysbroeck, but he uses Ruysbroeck's own terms when he teaches that grace issues from the unity of the faculties. God is closer to us than we are to ourselves and he acts on us from within, not from outside as creatures do; from this simple unity grace floods the faculties and makes her presence known by the resulting acts of virtue. One of the aspects of the spiritual life to which Vervoort returns most often is that God is met in the depths of the soul. All this is "authentic Ruysbroeck" to which Vervoort adds a Franciscan note. Particularly in the *Wilderness of the Lord*, in a lesser degree elsewhere, he mourns over the suffering Christ, over the blood-boltered head, the bruised shoulders, the five wounds, just as had been done before him by the anonymous author of *Indica mihi* and by the Friar Minor John Brugman (d. 1473), who wrote a life of Christ[14] in 232 meditations.

Herp had great influence also on the Capuchin John Evangelist (d. 1635) who, unlike most of his fellow countrymen, owed much to seventeenth-century France, and notably to Benet of Canfield*. His book *God's Reign in You* makes him in a way the doctor of introversion, as his fellow friar, Luke of Malines (d. 1652), was certainly its poet. (See his *Glad Requiem, Sad Alleluia*, and *Cloister of the Spiritual Resurrection*[15]).

Another *milieu* open to Ruysbroeck's influence was that of the Beguines. In 1535 Thierry Loer van Straten, a Carthusian at Cologne who died nineteen years later, published the *Gospel Pearl*; it was reprinted in 1536; then, finding that his text was incomplete, the editor in 1538 published the first integral edition, under the title *The Great Gospel Pearl*. It was so successful that Loer van Straten gave up a project on which he had been working for some time, namely, the translation into Netherlandish of Tauler's sermons: for it seemed to him that Tauler's doctrine was effectively presented in the *Gospel Pearl*. The work did not stop there; when Loer left Cologne in 1542 or a little before, the spiritual director of the beguinage at Diest, Nicholas van Esch or Esschius (d. 1578), took it up. He published another work by the same writer, *The Temple*

* Who was in fact an Englishman, William Fitch of Little Canfield, Essex. He was one of the first two Capuchins in England, and wrote a famous treatise *On the Holy Will of God* (*The Rule of Perfection*). See L. C. Sheppard in the *Downside Review*, Summer 1951, pp. 323-32. Father Benet died in 1610.

*Translator's note.*

*of the Soul*[16], and gave the first particulars—the only ones that are trustworthy—about the author's identity: he says she was a holy woman who died in 1540 at the age of seventy-seven. Nicholas so multiplied editions of the *Gospel Pearl* that the one issued at Antwerp in 1629 was already the twelfth, and in the meantime there had been Latin, French and German translations, in 1545, 1602 and 1676 respectively. The names of the translators alone were enough to recommend the book to people's notice: they were the Carthusians Lawrence Surius (d. 1578) and Richard Beaucousin (d. 1610), who was the spiritual director of Bérulle, and the German poet John Scheffler (d. 1677), who is better known by his pen-name of Angelus Silesius. One has only to read a few chapters here and there among the 168 that make up *Gospel Pearl* to find out that its spirituality is centred in the person of Christ. It is, however, not enough to follow him in his joys and sorrows—they must become as it were our own. This "Christiform" life can be found only in mystical union with our head, that Christ with whom we form one single body and from whom the soul receives such varied gifts. Thanks to this union with our Lord in faith and love we live the different states and conditions of his life: his gladness and his grief become ours, his virtues and his merits become in some sort ours, for the life of the head is the life of the whole body. If we understand the meaning of the *Gospel Pearl* aright, these "Christiform" persons will always have a joyous spirit, in union with their Lord who even at his moment of greatest dereliction was still one with the Father; they will always be sad in soul, in union with their Lord who is wounded by man's ingratitude beyond the ability of words to express; they will always be afflicted in body, in union with their Lord who endured so many wants and torments in his body.

This "Christiform" life depends on a mystical birth of Christ in the soul, which the authoress of the *Gospel Pearl* sees under three different aspects, namely, an enlightening of the mind, the inpouring of the supernatural virtues and the irradiation of the bodies of the righteous by the mystical life which our Lord lives in them. And she brings these three mystical births into association with the three Masses of Christmas-day, reminding the reader more than once that our Lady was the first who underwent this experience.

Whoever has some acquaintance with Ruysbroeck's works will readily agree that the Christocentric orientation of the *Pearl* cannot be found in them. It may even be said that in Ruysbroeck's time Christocentrism was still in a stage of growth, and the slightest familiarity with his writings is enough to show that in them Christocentrism has a far lesser place than in the *Gospel Pearl*. At the same time its authoress does not ignore the hidden things of the life of the Triune God, the return of the predestined under the shelter of the Word to the bosom of the Father, self-recollection in the depths of the soul, direct sight of the divine essence.   For all that she mentions his name only once, most of this is owed to Ruysbroeck and for this reason the authoress of the *Gospel Pearl* ranks with Henry Herp as one of the chief factors in the diffusion of Ruysbroeck's teaching among the mystics of the "counter-reformation".

It is no matter for surpise that when Nicholas van Esch wrote his *Exercitia spiritualia* (first edition in 1548) he was in the first place under the influence of the writings of his pupil. This book is concerned with the "Christiform life"; Nicholas gives more attention to the ascetic elements that condition it than does his exemplar, but the simpler style and seeming ascetical preoccupation must not be allowed to mislead us about its source and real subject.

The authoress of the *Gospel Pearl* did not say the last word on our Lord's part in mystical experience; about a century later another Beguine, Claesinne van Nieuwlant (d. 1611), made further contributions to the subject. A highly-respected spiritual director of the day, Peregrine Pullen (d. 1608), visited this woman in the beguinage at Ghent in order to learn from her, and the minutes of their conversation have survived.[17] Claesinne said that the contemplative is so lost in God that it is God himself who contemplates God in the human soul, which in some sense becomes God. The price of this is a complete and utter renunciation: renunciation of the understanding, for the soul knows God only in not-knowing, outside all human concepts; renunciation of the will, of all practice of the virtues measured by our limited and fundamentally egocentric being. Such an emptying-out of self by the aspirant towards mystical experience involves a correspondingly unreserved union with the person of Christ. God can be known in Christ, and only in him. No one knows the Father except the Son, and those to whom the Son reveals him. The Son reveals the Father only to those in whom the Father is well-pleased. And since the Father is solely and only well-pleased with the Son, we are not well-pleasing to him in as much as we are not in the Son. And we can be in the Son only if we live with the life of Jesus Christ.

Those are only a few elements of a spirituality which in every way deserves deep and careful study. And the points picked up in conversation by an enlightened questioner are amply sufficient to show that at the end of the sixteenth century there were souls in the Netherlands beguinages whose elevation of thought and state of renunciation were worthy of the days of Hadewijch.

As Nicholas van Esch owed much to the writer of the *Gospel Pearl*, so did Pullen to Claesinne van Nieuwlant. The new creature or new man of whom he speaks in *The Book of the New Creature*[18] is the contemplative who has reached that state of union with God that Ruysbroeck calls union without difference. This Pullen sees in two aspects, identification with

E

the Triune God and identification with Christ (the first being grafted on to the second), and this "identification" is of course mystical, not ontological. For Pullen, Christ's contribution to the act of contemplation is much more than simply being a model by whom we must be inspired if we would reach the preparatory level necessary as a prerequisite to supernatural contemplation. It is precisely in the Word and thanks to him that we must attain contemplation, for we become "deiform" only by living in the "deiformity" of Christ. Our Lord, then, is the prism through which we contemplate God, and any contemplation which claims to do otherwise is only a deceitful fancy. Pullen is careful to remind his readers that Christ's manhood is part of this quasi-formal reason of the act of contemplation.

The divine essence seems to be the adequate object of contemplation in Pullen's thought, and even more than Ruysbroeck he is constrained to explain so sublime a contemplation by the light of the Word here functioning as "kind". Finally, Pullen is at one with Hadewijch, Appelmans and Ruysbroeck in emphasizing the apostolic significance of the work of contemplation. Because of his union with Christ, the contemplative's actions breathe Christ without his suspecting it.

So, although he makes no reference to him, Peregrine Pullen took up the teaching of Ruysbroeck, as well as of the authoress of the *Gospel Pearl*, and completed them both. Indeed, it may be said that, so far as the Low Countries are concerned, it was he who drew up the credo of Christocentric spirituality. He made of the "Christiform" life as taught by the writer of the *Gospel Pearl* something much more than a prerequisite disposition to contemplation that it was for Ruysbroeck. The contemplative must contemplate with Christ's eyes; he will catch a glimpse of God in and through Christ.

This sketch would be very incomplete if we failed to mention Louis de Blois (d. 1566), who lived nearly fifty years before

Pullen and Claesinne van Nieuwlant.* He spent most of his life as abbot of the Benedictine monastery at Liessies, near Avesnes in the diocese of Cambrai, and he was also born and brought up in the Low Countries; and the collection of his quotations from Ruysbroeck published by M. Magnus in 1876[19] showed that he was one of the contemplatives who drew most heavily on that source. His spiritual teaching is difficult to summarize, for, apart from the *Institutio spiritualis*, his writings are remarkably undidactic.

It may however be said that Louis de Blois was the doctor of the divine presence—putting aside the bookish connotation of that phrase. His theology was summed up in that presence, and he regarded it as the only sure and sage way for whoever hungers after holiness. The Christian who wants to progress in the knowledge of God must begin by withdrawing to the innermost recess of his own soul, and this state of recollection should become the only atmosphere in which he can breathe normally. There he will experience a first union with God, the union of those who with a quiet and humble love rely on God's presence within themselves; there he will find that union of simple conformity to God's will which leads on towards the heights of renunciation. Such expressions, found in the *Speculum spirituale*, are calculated to encourage any Christian of good will. But this union can be realized only at the foot of the Cross; we can train ourselves in renunciation only in the school of the Crucified, pondering the lessons for our life hidden in the story of our Saviour's passion: and it was to help us to do this that Louis de Blois, under the inspiration of Tauler, wrote the *Dominicae Passionis explicatio*. Though having a basis of introversion, the spirituality of Louis de Blois is Christocentric, and it is no surprise to find him insisting on a further union, the sacramental union with our Lord in the

* In England Louis de Blois is better known as Blosius.
                                        *Translator's note.*

Eucharist: his whole position can be summed up in the words "From the Eucharist to the Trinity". Those are the two pillars of fire that light the way; the Christian life is worked out between those two dogmas. The first is the indispensable food for our journey; the second is the object of our burning desires, of which momentary glimpses are granted to those souls who are purified by renunciation. These sublime "touches" are the privilege arising from that mystical union of spirit with spirit wherein the one becomes the other no more than white-hot iron becomes fire. In his later works, *Speculum spirituale*, *Consolatio pusillanimium*, *Divini amoris igniariolum*, Louis de Blois multiplies aspirations towards union with Holy Trinity; this is the ardent consummation of a spirituality that is conceived in introversion and develops in the most authentic Christocentrism.

Of all the disciples of Ruysbroeck with whom we have been concerned in this chapter Louis de Blois is the one who shows least interest in the philosophical bases of the soul's union with God. He does not ignore them altogether, but he does not want the understanding to be taken up with metaphysics at the expense of the heart; so he simplifies philosophical doctrine and gives it a much more affective turn. This simplicity and warmth of tone, most attractive to the reader, is Louis de Blois's Benedictine contribution to the heritage he received from Ruysbroeck.

While the Franciscans, among others, were concerned with the person of Christ, the Carmelites (better known in times past in the Low Countries as Friars of the Virgin) emphasized more than had been done before our Lady's part in mystical experience—without, of course, in any way falsifying the true order of values. The principal writers to be mentioned in this connection are Michael-of-St-Augustine and his pupil Mary-of-St-Teresa, who may be called the two doctors of the "Mariform" life.

Michael-of-St-Augustine (d. 1684) says several times, in the *Devout Life in Christ* for example, that creatures can be considered in God in two ways. One way is that creatures are in their essence united with the ideas that are in God from all eternity, and these ideas are God's very essence. Michael, then, held a most authentic exemplarism, the exemplarism of Ruysbroeck; and he also knew his theory of the three unions, through intermediary, without intermediary, and essential union. But the "Mariform" life was something new. Michael understood it as contemplation having for its object both God and our Lady, as he who contemplates Christ considers at the same time in him both God and man ; it drew its perfection from the union of our Lady with God, a union more perfect than that known by any other creature. The best means for progressing in this life are not the same for all: for some it would be consideration of the many graces with which Mary was endowed; for others, a love for her so tender that it may be called melting. Michael reminds us that the spirit of Christ inspires in the soul a love of his Mother just as it inspires a love of God the Father; all graces come to us through her mediation, and therefore union with God in and through our Lady is more complete than it is without this Marian element.

There is an obvious connection between this idea of the "Mariform" life and the spirituality of St Louis Grignion de Montfort, who was some forty years younger than Michael-of-St-Augustine. Michael's friary at Brussels belonged to the Touraine observance, and it is very likely that the Carmelites of Rennes, where the Touraine reform originated, had copies of his books, which were published, more or less simultaneously in Latin and in Netherlandish, between 1659 and 1671. Now it is known that St Louis Grignion de Montfort frequented the Carmelite house at Rennes in his youth, and this surely is the reason for the resemblances in doctrine, and even in vocabulary, between the writings of the Dominican tertiary

and the Brussels Carmelite; the resemblances are not accidental: St Louis was the debtor of Michael-of-St-Augustine.

But the views of Michael are themselves not entirely
original, and the autobiographical notes of Mary-of-St-Teresa
(d. 1677), which he edited, show that he was considerably
indebted to her. This Carmelite recluse of Malines whose
name "in the world" was Mary Petyt, was born at Hazebroeck;
she must be distinguished from another Carmelite Mary-of-
St-Teresa whose letters were published in Paris in 1720, who
was born in the Bordeaux country. For Mary Petyt the
"Mariform" life began with the diligent consideration of our
Lady's life and virtues, and this unremitting meditation enabled her to leave sensible devotion behind without repressing
the promptings of the emotions; it also enabled her to learn
that the source of these virtues was our Lady's union with
God. Thenceforward she saw our Lady as the great contemplative, the mistress of all life of prayer: not simply a model
to be followed but a teacher to be humbly listened to. The
French translator of the pertinent pages of Mary Petyt[20]
expounds with careful judgement how the soul finds more
satisfaction in our Lady's union with God than in its own;
union with him in and through her lifts our life to her level,
without our losing consciousness of our own personal union
with God. Mary Petyt calls this "union without intermediary"
—in a sense very different from Ruysbroeck's use of the
expression—and it is brought about by a fusion of love. Nor
is the "Mariform" life the last stage in the soul's ascent.
There comes a time when it is so transformed in our Lady
that like her it has direct contact with Jesus Christ, and so
with God. The soul's union with our Lady is then in a virtual
and eminent way embodied in the union of the soul with God.

It may be objected that it is very dangerous to hold the
possibility of a union more perfect than union with God. But
Mary-of-St-Teresa reminds us that an accidental glory is

added to the essential glory of some of the blessed in Heaven, and that this in no wise detracts from the excellence of that essential glory which is the lot of all the blessed without distinction. Nor was this "Mariform" spiritual life the result of a syllogism dictating a way of prayer hitherto unknown; Mary Petyt was very little concerned with theorizing: her opinions about mystical experience, about the Marian life in particular, developed parallel with her own visions, revelations and illuminations. That is why her spiritual director, Michael-of-St-Augustine, obviously got from her almost everything that he tells us about the "Mariform" life. Mary Petyt's doctrine on this subject is clearer and more complete than Michael's; on the other hand, she probably took from him what she says about the depths of the soul, the spiritual spark, and other reminiscences of Ruysbroeck.

It was not only members of religious orders founded in the middle ages or earlier who followed in the furrow Ruysbroeck had drawn. The leaders of the noble Society of Jesus showed no great interest in the mystics, but some of its early members were very devoted to Ruysbroeck's writings. An outstanding example is St Peter Canisius (d. 1597) whose real name was Peter Dhondt.* Soon after becoming a Jesuit he published, in 1543 and under Tauler's name, a collection of texts which he called *The True Evangelical Life: Divine Sermons, Teachings, Letters, Songs and Prophecies*. The second part of this collection, better known by the name *Institutiones Taulerianae*, consists of Netherlandish and Rhenish writings, including important extracts from Ruysbroeck.

There was also Leonard Lessius (d. 1623) who, while he was a professor at the theological college at Louvain, won himself a name in the course of the controversies that went on over the teachings of Baius. But Lessius was not only a doughty

---

* *Canis* translates *Dhondt*. He was born at Nÿmegen.
                                                      *Translator's note.*

controversialist: he was also a man of deep spirituality, and his treatise *De summo Bono*[21] shows how well read he was in Ruysbroeck's work and doctrine.

And again there was Maximilian Sandaeus (d. 1651), who was specially worried by the notoriously disparate terminology of the mystics. With the idea of reducing it to order he published in 1640 his *Clavis Theologiae mysticae*[22]; it was perhaps before its time, but it was a learned work and prompted by a concern for lexicographical exactness that is unusual. That Sandaeus was interested in the spirituality of Ruysbroeck is shown by the numerous terms mentioned which were due to him and his followers, such as *vita superessentialis, unio sine medio, unio sine differentia*. These terms were the occasion for the giving of some of the pertinent passages in the *Clavis Theologiae mysticae*, so that Sandaeus was one of those who gave testimony for Ruysbroeck to the seventeenth century.

This enquiry need be carried no further. From the early years of the eighteenth century mystical literature was in a decline. Bossuet died in 1704. But the Catholic Church always has her saints, even in the darkest times; and it is no surprise to find true followers of Ruysbroeck right in the eighteenth century. Charles Grimminck (d. 1728), parish priest of Zuidcote and of Caestre, near Ypres, and then a hermit at the foot of the Mont-des-Cats, left works written partly in Netherlandish and partly in Latin, and some in French, of which the integral publication is still to come[23]. In those parts that have been printed, we find Grimminck referring to a clear contemplation of God amid the dark "clouds of unknowing". In the course of mystical experience souls pass into the un-created and ideal being in which they were from all eternity, without however losing their created being. These things happen by way of love, and Grimminck by preference explains them by the analogy of melting. The question whether he had read Ruysbroeck is beside the point. Whoever were the previous writers who may have influenced him, it is clear that, when early in the eighteenth century Charles Grimminck looked for a philosophical explanation of theopathic states, he found it in Ruysbroeck's thesis of the return of the soul into God, on a foundation of exemplarism.


# REFERENCES

[1] The best edition of this work is that in which Abbé André Combes gives as well other pieces from the Ruysbroeck-Gerson dossier, and that is the one used here. *Essai sur la critique de Ruysbroeck par Gerson*, in the series *Études de théologie et d'histoire de la spiritualité, fasc. IV* (Paris, 1945), t. I, pp. 716–71.

[2] *Gerardi Magni Epistolae*, ed. W. Mulder, S.J. (coll. *Tekstuitgaven van Ons Geestelijk Erf*, fasc. III), Antwerp, 1933; p. 208.

[3] *De phasen van het mystieke leven*, in *Ons Geestelijk Erf*, t. VIII (1934), pp. 21–8.

[4] *Het toppunt der beschouwing naar Jan van Leeuwen*, in *Ons Geestelijk Erf*, t. IX (1935), pp. 29–60.

[5] John van Leeuwen's warm praise of Hadewijch and his diatribe against Eckhart show that the library at Groenendael possessed the works of these writers; otherwise a man of limited learning such as the cook could hardly have known what they had written.

[6] Apart from one or two booklets, only extracts from the writings of John van Leeuwen have been published. Only one manuscript of his complete works is known, and by mistake its two volumes bear different numbers. They are catalogued mss. Brussels, Bibliothèque royale 667 and 888–90. The Dominican library at Lierre in Belgium has a manuscript, fifty years older than the Brussels one, which corresponds to B.B.R.667 and contains nine of John van Leeuwen's works.

[7] *Doctoris ecstatici D. Dionysii Cartusiani Opera omnia . . .* (Montreuil, 1896–1913).

[8] *De Contemplatione*, lib. III, art. 14; ed. *Opera omnia*, t. XLI, p. 270A'.

[9] The same, p. 227A' and 111B'.

[10] *Jan van Ruusbroec, Leven, Werken* (Amsterdam, 1931), pp. 235-48.

[11] Antwerp, 1551.

[12] Louvain, 1552.

[13] Antwerp, 1566.

[14] *Johannes Brugman en het godsdienstig leven onzer vaderen in de vijftiende eeuw*, ed. Moll (Amsterdam, 1854), t. II, pp. 287-407.

[15] For the works of Luke of Malines, see the editions of Antwerp, 1631, and of Ghent, 1674.

[16] Antwerp, 1543.

[17] *Markante mystiek in het Gentsch begijnhof, Claesinne van Nieuwlant*, in *Ons Geestelijk Erf*, t. XIII (1939), pp. 291-360 and 403-44.

[18] *Pullen's tractaatje 'Van een nieuwe creature'*, in *Ons Geestelijk Erf*, t. I (1944), pp. 196-212.

[19] *Lichtstrahlen aus den Schriften Katholiker Mystiker* (Munich, 1876) t. II.

[20] *L'union mystique à Marie par Marie de Sainte-Thérèse* tr. L. van den Bossche, fasc. 15 of *Les Cahiers de la Vierge* (Juvisy, n.d.), p. 17.

[21] *Leonardi Lessii . . . Opuscula* (Antwerp, 1626), pp. 487-615.

[22] Cologne, 1640.

[23] Raphaël Persyn, *Un mystique flamand, Charles Grimminck*, (1676-1728), *Contribution à l'histoire religieuse de la Flandre* (coll. *Éditions du Comité flamand de France*), Lille-Paris-Lyon, 1925.

# CHAPTER IV

## THE "DEVOTIO MODERNA"

THE great dependence of the speculative spirituality of
the Low Countries on Ruysbroeck is a commonplace;
but the emphasizing of his influence on such as Herp and
Denis van Rijkel has too often ended in a judgement that the
more practical stream of spirituality, the *Devotio moderna*, is
the most incompatible with his ideas. And so it comes about
that those who claim him for German spirituality look on
*Devotio moderna* as the sole spirituality of the Low Countries,
while those who do not want to give him up say that Netherlandish spirituality has two fundamentally divergent aspects,
the speculative school of Ruysbroeck and the practical school
of the Brethren of the Common Life. To us it seems that what
separates *Devotio moderna* from the spirituality of Brabant is
a matter of proportional composition: when the chief exponents of *Devotio moderna* treat of mystical experience they
follow Ruysbroeck—but they do not treat of it often.

Gerard Groote (d. 1384) was undeniably the promoter of
the practical school that contemporaries there and then labelled
the "new devotion". And it is most significant that he once
declared his great appreciation of the spirit of Ruysbroeck,
and several times went to Groenendael to refresh his own soul.
It is true that Groote was much less a mystical writer than
many others. He was above all the doughty champion of that
reform of personal life which was becoming more and more
important, and most of his works were written with a view to
getting rid of the disorders amid which a weary clergy and a
crippled laity were floundering. It would therefore be foolish
to imagine those writings to be even a passably adequate

expression of Groote's spirituality. It is much better to look for that in the way of life of the Brothers and Sisters of the Common Life, and in the daily rule of the canons regular of Windesheim. During the closing years of the fourteenth century compunction took the place of metaphysics in the spiritual life of the Low Countries, and this was in great measure due to the influence of Gerard Groote. For evidence of this it is enough to read one or other of his letters, such as that to Matthias Tyla in 1382 or the one he wrote, at the beginning of 1384, to a religious whose nerves were upest (known as the *Epistola de patientia*[1]).

There was give as well as take between Groote and Groenendael: John van Schoonhoven, for instance, inherited some of his spirit. Schoonhoven came to Groenendael in 1374, and soon earned the confidence of some of his fellows. After he had read the *Adornment of the Spiritual Marriage*, in the Latin translation of William Jordaens, Gerson made some very definite reservations about book III; and it was Schoonhoven who was entrusted with the defence of Ruysbroeck's orthodoxy, and his *Epistola responsalis* (1408)[2] is still the best plea in this cause. Schoonhoven undertakes to show that in the impugned passages Ruysbroeck is concerned neither with the fusion of two beings into one by suppression of the identity of one of them, nor with a moral unity brought about by the conformity of two wills. It is rather union by a melting and ecstasy that he finds characteristic of the mystical life. This teaching can claim support from fathers of the Church, from Dionysius "the Areopagite", from St Thomas Aquinas. Of course there are some who say that St Thomas's teaching has nothing to do with Ruysbroeck's lucubrations; but they should not be too sure. In explanation of Ruysbroeck's idea of the soul's union with God, Schoonhoven invokes St Thomas's doctrine of the divine essence "informing" the created understanding in the Beatific Vision; and, in spite of certain necessary cautions, this collocation of doctrines has a good deal to be said for it.

It would seem that this explanation of Ruysbroeck's most difficult pages made an impression at the time, and Schoonhoven refers to it in one of his sermons. After the reunion of the Brabant monasteries to the Windesheim congregation in 1413 a general chapter was held and John van Schoonhoven was invited to preach the capitular sermon. This sermon *Fiet unum ovile et unus pastor*[3] seems to have been much to the taste of the Windesheim religious, for Schoonhoven was asked to preach at their meetings on several subsequent occasions. The second time, in the sermon *Venite ascendamus ad montem Domini*, he took the ascent of Mount Horeb as representing the mystical life, and it certainly seems that he expected to find at its height St Paul's face-to-face vision.

Schoonhoven did not let success go to his head, and this second capitular sermon was the last in which he ventured to talk about mystical experience. It may well be believed that actual contact with people convinced him that, for most religious, ascetical problems were much more important than mystical doctrine; and he referred to it only incidentally in the two capitular sermons that followed (*Nos autem gloriari oportet* and *Videte quomodo caute ambuletis*), and in his other sermons and letters of direction. This does not mean that these other writings are at all lacking in interest: his modest observations are marked with a rare wisdom, though they have a certain impersonality of tone due to the large number of quotations from other authors. In the *Epistola prima in Eemsteyn*, written to his nephew Simon, V. Becker[4] has detected phrases of which echoes can be heard in the *Imitation of Christ*. Schoonhoven, then, is an excellent ascetical writer. The question is, whether the interest in mysticism that he shows from time to time is due to his own experiences, or whether it is simply the concern of a theologian worrying over the problem of a direct vision of God. The fact that in his second capitular sermon he claims such a vision for several contemporary holy persons suggests that the second hypothesis is right[5]. If so, John van Schoonhoven was a supporter of Ruysbroeck rather than a disciple formed in his likeness.

But the spirit of Gerard Groote was to be found principally in the houses of the Brothers and Sisters of the Common Life. These were projected by Groote himself, and their realization was entrusted to Florent Radewijns (d. 1400), who founded the first houses of men. As a writer he was mediocre, and all that survives is a few selections of lecture notes. The canons regular of the Windesheim congregation seem to have been a more cultured body, and it was among them above all that there was a literary activity enabling us to follow the spiritual development of the Low Countries.

There was, for instance, Gerlac Peters (d. 1411), who joined the Windesheim community before 1400. In his *Soliloquium* he lines up with Ruysbroeck's exemplarism. Chapter XXVII shows how God uninterruptedly contemplates his eternal image in us. Chapter VIII is clearer still, for it shows how the soul united with God can abstract from all created images in the contemplation of Truth and Superessence in every created being. Elsewhere Peters says that when God's look meets ours there ceases to be any intermediary, in a certain fashion anyway; and in explaining this he twice uses Ruysbroeck's figure of white-hot iron. But he is careful to stress that in this union the soul never loses its own identity, which always remains distinct from God.

Like Ruysbroeck, Peters teaches that this union takes place in the soul's essence, and accordingly he calls the fruition that follows union a pure and essential fruition of simple truth. His mysticism also has a trinitarian orientation, the soul in its own way becoming conformed to the Holy Trinity through its three powers. But this element is far less developed in Peters than in Ruysbroeck.

Gerlac Peters has a special place among Ruysbroeck's disciples and seems to have been the most faithful to his master's mystical doctrine among his brethren. But the atmosphere of the *Soliloquium* is very different from that of Ruysbroeck's writings. Though professing exemplarism, Peters admits that it had less interest for him than the consideration of his own nothingness. He was more concerned about compunction of heart, all that it involves and all that gets in the way of its attainment; and so, though it is not very happy to call him *alter Thomas a Kempis*, he was one of his forerunners. Father Puyol[6], an authority on the "Imitation", says that nearly all parts of Peter's writings can be paralleled by some passage or other of the "Imitation". When Gerlac Peters died in 1411 this book had not yet been published.

But it was at the beginning of this fifteenth century that Thomas a Kempis (d. 1471) first took up his pen. When he joined the canons regular of Mount St Agnes in 1399 he began a monastic and literary career that was to last for nearly seventy-three years. His writings were numerous; of the forty which Pohl collected into his critical edition there are three which stand out because of the direct and personal way in which they deal with the interior life: these are the *Soliloquium*, the *De elevatione mentis ad inquirendum summum bonum*, and the four treatises which together bear the title *De imitatione Christi*.

At first sight the *Soliloquium* seems to treat of union with God, to whom the soul must cling; it begins with the 28th verse of Psalm lxxii: "Mihi autem adhaerere Deo bonum est". But the atmosphere of the book proves to be not that of the unitive way; it is too concerned with sin for that. Union with God is seen only through the prism of our shortcomings: Kempis fidgets impatiently at the threshold of the sanctuary, but is too troubled by consciousness of his failings to be able to go in. The *Soliloquium* is a book of homesickness.

The style of the *Imitation of Christ* is like that of the *Soliloquium*, it uses rime, *cursus* and parallelism; but it displays a much greater maturity of soul. Who wrote the four treatises that bear this common title? The author himself replies that it is less important to know who wrote a book than to know what is its worth as a spiritual work. But for a long time historians and philologists have been of another opinion, and the dispute about the authorship of the *Imitation* is still not quite played out. One has only to study the atmosphere in which the Windesheim canons lived and wrote to see at once the author was not Gerson the Chancellor or his shadow, Gersen the ghost; or for that matter almost any other of the forty or so candidates who have been put forward. Nor did Gerard Groote write it; but it is none the less imbued with his spirit.

The reader of the *Imitation* finds in Thomas a Kempis a particularly sensitive soul, one for whom the monastic life was not easy but who managed to use his disappointments as a ladder by which to climb ever higher in the way of self-renunciation. He was hurt by the community that he did not feel big enough to stand up to; but suffering taught him to understand better what Christ asks from each one of us, as well as the resources at hand for those called to the life of the cloister. The first book of the *Imitation* begins with a declaration of the emptiness of all human values, and after disavowing wealth, honours, delight of the senses, long life, Kempis devotes two chapters to the vanity of human knowledge. It looks as if either he himself had put too much trust in such knowledge at the beginning of his religious life or else he had had a close-up view of the excesses of certain teachers; in any case he was blaming the exaggerations of a degenerate scholasticism. The whole of the first book is given up to renunciation. Book II is much more directly an initiation into the inner life. The kingdom of God is within us and it is only within ourselves that we find him. But to do so we must keep out all intruders. Such a point of view is the only one that can be taken by an experienced man. All human affection fails sooner or later, God's friendship alone is enduring; and so henceforth Thomas a Kempis urges us to lend a ready ear to God's entreaties. Certain things are required before we can answer the Master's call: humility, inner peace, purity of intention, careful watch over our instincts, an exact conscience, love for Jesus at times of distress as at times of happiness—those are the chief dispositions that make the soul able to correspond with the movements of Jesus.

The third book is nearly as long as the other three put together, and it is the book of friendship: references to the love of Jesus, hitherto only touched on, become the material of the work. From the beginning Kempis follows the way of introversion (though he does not use that term). If she would hear God's call, the soul must withdraw into herself; and in this state of recollection from which the world is excluded, there takes place that converse between Master and disciple whose content reveals a religious insight up till then unknown to the devout. " Listen, my son, for what I have to tell you is far beyond the learning of the philosohpers and wise men of all the ages. My words are inspiration and life . . .". " Happy is the man taught by you, Lord . . .". "My son, whoever walks before me in the truth need fear no assault . . .". "My son, your love is not yet strong enough or enlightened enough". "Why, Lord?" "Because you leave the work you have put your hand to at the slightest difficulty".

The presentation in this third book is rather different from that of the preceding ones, as befits the greater delicacy of its matter. The chapters continue the dialogue form, which is specially well adapted to the themes treated. Whatever way one may prefer, Thomas a Kempis takes the indications of Jesus Himself, which specially receptive souls still receive in

F

their prayer to-day. "My son, when grace prompts you to devout acts, it is better for you and safer to keep that grace hidden . . .". "My son, if you want to be happy, take me for your last and highest end . . .". "My son, the man who tries to withdraw himself from obedience withdraws himself from grace; . . . and he who wants to own something loses that which is everybody's . . .". "Your sufferings are slight compared with those of so many others . . .". "My son, set yourself to do another's will, rather than your own . . .". "Renounce yourself, my son, and you will find yourself . . .". But it is needless to go on quoting. Enough has been said to show what understanding Kempis had of Christ's soul, so eager for friendship.

Finally, the fourth book, which is not exactly on the same lines as the others, though the master ideas of the third are therein transposed and adapted to eucharistic devotion—that Christian devotion *par excellence*. But this identity of themes must not be exaggerated, and the fourth book has not the "discreetly autobiographical" turn that certainly seems to be found in the first three.[7] The whole work can be summed up as the book of intimacy with Jesus conditioned by absolute renouncement of self, and in writing it Kempis was mindful of the store of experience available in those who had gone before him. Groote and several of his followers used to keep a *rapiarium*, "commonplace book", in which they wrote down thoughts and quotations that struck them during their reading. These *rapiaria* were extensively used in their own work, and Thomas a Kempis manifestly arranged and completed these collections, altering and improving them with a touch that was as delicate as it was sure. In this way Gerard Groote, Schoonhoven, Radewijns, Gerlac Peters and the rest all wrote the *Imitation*, or rather certain parts of it; and so, the whole brought together by Thomas a Kempis, it represents the best in the contribution of the Low Countries to Christian spirituality.

It is not exact to say that mystical experience is unknown to the *Imitation*; but it is quite true that this book is about the way which leads to union with Jesus Christ rather than about that union itself, which is the subject of *De elevatione mentis ad inquirendum summum bonum*. Here Kempis seeks God outside and above intellectual concepts, "super rationes intellectuales", and such expressions as "tui capacem" and "aeternae veritatis capacem" suggest that he believed such union to be attainable, with the help of grace. His way is that of Ruysbroeck's introversion, and he does not fail to dwell on the peace and consolation of this close attachment to the Word. There seems to be nothing in the writings of Thomas a Kempis which enables us to decide whether this expression, " attachment to the Word", is to be understood as the report of one who had experienced a direct vision or whether it looks forward to that state of imminent glory which is known by some who have reached great spiritual maturity. But, if it must be interpreted with reference to a passage about the uncreated light that Kempis longs to see in the light of God, it would seem that the retrospective interpretation is less in disaccord with the text. This superessential light recalls the "essentia divina in suo proprio lumine videnda" of John van Schoonhoven.

It cannot then be maintained that Kempis hardly appreciated the problem of mystical experience. On the contrary, he had a better appreciation of it than had many other writers, but he believed that ascetical matters were of more significance for the general run of his readers. As has been said above, the *Imitation* establishes the stages of renunciation which are prerequisite to divine union; the *De elevatione mentis* is concerned with union itself. In the first Kempis is the more human, in the second he may be likened to the divine doctor John van Ruysbroeck. But the *Imitation* is by far the better book: like so many great books, it was the offspring of a synthesis of matter and spirit, of enthusiasm and sacrifice.

The compunction cultivated by the followers of Gerard Groote was not, however, the whole of the more practical spirituality of the fifteenth century. For many at that time the following of Christ soon became union with Jesus, and this was one of the most effective factors in promoting the mystical impulse that moved religious life under the influence of *Devotio moderna*. This is illustrated by the *Epistola de vita et passione Domini nostri Jhesu Christi*[8], strongly recommended to his subjects by John Vos van Heusden (d. 1424), prior of Windesheim: this *Epistola* consisted mainly of meditations for each day of the week such as were beginning to be known at that time.

But let us make no mistake. It was above all the Franciscans who, following their beloved founder St Francis of Assisi, stimulated devotion to the suffering Christ. From the beginning of the fifteenth century there were some for whom compunction passed into compassion for the tortured Saviour: they sought to be hidden in Christ's wounds, to find in them the honey of devotion; they wished to share his indignities and blows. They were enraptured by the beauty of the most beautiful among the sons of men. It seemed to them that the sole of Christ's foot was more sensitive to pain than the eye of an ordinary man—and what more sensitive than the eye?[9] And so when we read John Brugman's sermons (d. 1473) or the collection called *Indica mihi*[10] or the treatises of Francis Vervoort (d. 1555) we find more and more pathos and tears and ecstasy; and to attribute them to literary affectation is to fail to understand the spirit of the age.

It was in order to re-live each moment of the passion that the priest Peter Sterckx (or Potens), on returning from the Holy Land, set up at Louvain in 1505 a way of the cross of seven stations. The principal elements of the Flemish formula of the way of the cross were brought together by a Carmelite of Malines, John van Paeschen (d. after 1532)[11]; these were put in order by a priest of Delft, Christian van Adrichem (or Adrichomius; d. 1585)[12]; and, according to the Jerusalem topographers, Father H. Vincent, O.P., and Father M. Abel, O.P.[13], the Church made them her own during the seventeenth century. It is clear that the way of the cross is the Franciscan devotion to the suffering Christ as recommended by the Church to all Christians. And we can see that for the Franciscans of the Low Countries it provided one more opportunity to follow their founder in what Father Rousselot[14] once called the ecstatic way of love.

# REFERENCES

[1] *Gerardi Magni Epistolae*, ed. W. Mulder, ep. 27, pp. 119–21 and ep. 62, pp. 232–43.

[2] *Essai sur la critique de Ruysbroeck par Gerson*, ed. André Combes; t. I, pp. 716–71.

[3] The best manuscript of Schoonhoven is the one written at Groenendael only a little time after his death, *viz.*, MS. Brussels, Bibliothèque royale, 15129. It does not, however, contain all Schoonhoven's writings.

[4] *Een voorlooper van Thomas a Kempis*, in *Onze Wachter*, t. I. (1882), pp. 389–402.

[5] The passage is as follows: 'Celitus tamen ille paulus in statu comprehensoris quadammodo factus usque ad tercium celum, hoc est usque ad immediatam visionem Dei et beatorum spirituum raptum se fore humiliter gloriatur. Que etiam visio in quibusdam modernis sanctis nostri temporis facta fuisse et fieri minime dubitatur. Hii enim mentis simplicitate ac virtutis contemplative perspicua bonitate non nunquam sic extra se rapiuntur, quod totaliter absorbentur, et divinam essentiam revelata intelligentie facie, immediate quodammodo, prout est possibile, contemplantur', Sermo 'Venite ascendamus ad montem Domini', in MS. Brussels, Bibliothèque royale, 15129, f. 81r-v.

[6] *L'auteur du livre de Imitatione Christi* (Paris, 1899), p. 475.

[7] cfr. Pierre Debongnie, *Les thèmes de l'Imitation*, in *Revue d'Histoire ecclésiastique*, t. XXXVI (1940), p. 337.

[8] The *Epistola* was incorporated by the chronicler John Busch in the *Chronicon Windeshemense*, l. I, ch. 72. See *Des Augustiner-propstes Iohannes Busch Chronicon Windeshemense und Liber de reformatione monasteriorum*, ed. Karl Grube (*Geschichtsquellen der Provinz Sachsen und angrenzender Gebiete*, t. XIX), Halle, 1886; pp. 226–44.

[9] See the anonymous *Fasciculus Myrre*, Part I, ch. I (Antwerp, Hans van Liesvelt, s.d.).

[10] See the French translation by M. M. Saeyeys, *Indica mihi . . . Très pieuses méditations sur la Vie et la Passion du Christ, d'après un manuscrit du XVe siècle par un auteur franciscain inconnu, traduit du vieux flamand* (*Caritas*), Paris, 1926.

[11] See *La Pérégrination spirituelle vers la Terre Saincte et cité de Iérusalem, translatée en françoys par M. Nicolas de Leuze, dict de Fraxinis* (Douay, 1584).

[12] See *Theatrum Terrae sanctae* (Coloniae, 1590).

[13] *Jérusalem* (Paris, 1912–26); t. III, pp. 629–35.

[14] See *Pour l'histoire du problème de l'amour au moyen âge* (*Beiträge zur Geschichte der Philosophie des Mittelalters*, t. VI, f. 6), Münster, 1908, pp. 56–80.

# CHAPTER V

## IS THERE A LOW-COUNTRIES SPIRITUALITY?

A SPIRITUALITY characteristic of the Low Countries has been so often referred to in the preceding pages that the reader may well be startled by the question at the head of this chapter. But the question was put some years back by one whose competence in the field of the history of spirituality cannot be questioned, Father J. Huijben[1], and it is a question worth examination; it had been asked even before Father Huijben. In 1923 Tanquerey answered it in the affirmative. In a list of principal authors consulted, at the beginning of his *Précis de Théologie ascétique et mystique*[2] he divides medieval religious literature into six "schools", namely, Benedictine, Victorine, Dominican, Franciscan, Flemish and Carthusian. This division then is made partly on a basis of inheritance from the founders of religious orders and partly on a basis of nationality: and even the beginner in logic might accuse Tanquerey of sinning against the first rule of division thereby. In 1928 Edmund Bruggeman[3] also replied to our question in the affirmative. But to enable him to do that he had first of all excluded from Low Countries spirituality the work of such weighty writers as Denis the Carthusian Henry Herp, Nicholas van Esch, John Evangelist, Francis Vervoort and the authoress of *Gospel Pearl*. Such a drawing of lines at once raises suspicion.

Father Huijben, on the other hand, says "No"; in his opinion there is no such thing as a Flemish spirituality (a term we have preferred not to use), but rather at least half-a-dozen of them, of which he has tried in vain to find the common denominator. This finding caused excitement among historians of spirituality, and several declared they were unable to accept it; among them was the present writer.

One must go carefully, for it cannot be decided off-hand whether or no the country of origin of the feasts of the Holy Trinity and Corpus Christi, the devotions of the rosary and the stations of the cross in its present form, has its own proper spirituality. And first of all the terms of the discussion must be settled. By spirituality is meant in the first place mystical experience and the different forms of religious experience which lead up to it in one way or another. Gold that is bought and sold over the counter is not often 24-carat, it is generally alloyed with something else. So with spirituality. The spirituality of the mystics is a mixture of mystical experience and subsequent reflection; and that reflection and its expression are necessary, because mystical experience is in itself unutterable, literally beyond words. Nevertheless reflection is like the Trojan horse —it brings strangers into the city. That is to say, mystics in spite of themselves set forth some part of their personal experience in terms of learning previously acquired, which itself is not part of that experience. But they do not produce this learning just as it is found, for example, in articles in reviews: far from it. They do not regard everything they have read as having an equal value, and so in turn they interpret the previously-studied authors in terms of their strictly personal and incommunicable experience. What we commonly call such-and-such a mystic's spirituality is in fact the outcome of an osmosis, a compenetration between personal experience and previous reading, each modifying the over-positiveness of the other; and this outcome is often a body of doctrine. But this must be seen aright. So long as the mystical writer does not go in for a barren didacticism, like a school text-book, his teaching retains an atmosphere that conveys the sense of the lived realities. Nor, generally speaking, does it require any special skill to extract from an exposition that is simple and direct all the elements needed by one who understands only doctrinal systems. We must then be careful not to be misled by the way in which an inexpressible mystical experience is presented.

As for the spirituality of a whole people, it is the synthesis— when synthesis there is—of those things which the people's chief contemplatives acknowledge to be the most outstandingly important. When all the necessary *caveats* have been entered, the answer to the question of the existence of a Low-Countries spirituality is not a matter of incommunicable personal experience; it must be looked for in the field of the mystics' interpretation of that experience—a less personal affair. We prefer to speak of Low-Countries rather than Flemish or Netherlandish spirituality, because almost till the end of the middle ages the term "Flemish" had a much narrower application than it has to-day; Flemings then were not taken to include Brabanters and Frisians. As for "Netherlander", the word was not known as a proper name before the sixteenth century.

Having settled what our terms mean, we can turn to the different ways in which historians of spirituality have tried to deal with them. And first there is the geographical point of view, from which Father Huijben agrees that the Low Countries may be said to have their own spirituality. To it belong all those mystics who in the course of the centuries have passed their religious and writing life in those lands. In spite of the unwillingness of certain authors to commit themselves and of the definite denial of others, this means that Louis de Blois belonged to the Low-Countries spirituality: his French origin is much further off than the English origin of Benet of Canfield, who is well esteemed a proud possession of French literature. On the other hand, writers who belonged to the Low Countries only by birth, Guerric d'Igny and William de Saint-Thierry, for example, must be allotted to the countries in which they spent their religious lives. But geography can be understood in several ways and, if the geographical unity of a spirituality is to be anything more than a label, we must lay bare that human geography that lies beneath frontiers and boundaries. For those who look at the problem in this way, geographical unity coincides with ethno-psychological unity.

At first sight it does not seem that this coincidence need be unacceptable. To examine the matter in an ethno-psychological light requires that we should track down in the writings of the different mystics those traits of temperament which foreign travellers—Bartholomew the Englishman, Mabillon— from the thirteenth to the eighteenth century and since, have looked on as characteristic of our forefathers. Such an enquiry gives plenty of scope to the essayists. One of them will fish up the culinary allegory that some of our writers use, the mystical tavern and the feastings of the elect; in this they will see a transposition, "sublimation", of which the Flemings and Brabanters were in urgent need, for their truculence has had a reputation since the middle ages. Another will seize on the taste for metaphysics which was so pronounced in some of our authors (though the only notable philosopher in the Low Countries was a foreigner called Spinoza). This taste explains why our mystical writers paid so little attention to pathology. That pathological cases were not very rare is proved by the half-dozen followers of Herp who lost their reason through an excess of contemplation[4]; by the contemporary conviction, recorded by Henry Eger (d. 1408)[5], that in Carthusian monasteries the nervous system often became deranged after a short time; and by the diagnosis of neuroses of religious origin made by Peter Bloemeveen (d. 1536)[6]. The metaphysicians regarded pathology simply as a negligible contingency.

Plenty of other elements could be taken into consideration; indeed, this line of enquiry might well prove endless. The temperamental characteristics which travellers from abroad have attributed to the Flemings are not the same as those

which they profess to find among the Brabanters, the Frisians
or the Hollanders: one has only to read the *De Proprietatibus
rerum*,[7] that Bartholomew the Englishman wrote about 1250,
to be convinced of that. Regionalism then seems determined
to assert rights in the sanctuary of our spirituality. Some ask
whether, while certain psychical characteristics divide Flemings
from Brabanters and Frisians, there are not other traits which
bring together the seventeen provinces of the former Low
Countries into a passably homogeneous unity? This is a
question we need not go into at the moment. Whatever may
be the answer to it, it remains that temperamental characteristics common to all, or nearly all, the Low-Land provinces
could not be accepted as the elements in an ethno-psychological
unity unless they were found in secular literature as well. The
outcome of the ethno-psychological enquiry would always be
debatable for lack of sufficient influence on spirituality.

For those concerned with spirituality the things which
matter first of all are the theological point-of-view and the
psychical reactions that go with it; the unity and continuity
that are indispensable to all spiritually must first be looked
for in the field of doctrine. It is because this field is so often
regarded as closed that investigation gets nowhere. And
doctrine is not the only thing: there is an atmosphere, conditioned by devotions, observances, and tendencies of very
varying kinds. A comparison may help. If someone asks: "Is
there a Dominican spirituality?" we may well reply: "No,
there is not because there are several". At the root of Master
Eckhart's spirituality we find exemplarism, but we seek it in
vain in the work of St Catherine of Siena; Tauler dilates on
the basic will as recipient of the image of the Holy Trinity,
but Savonarola never mentions the subject. Though the two
meet in the work of Venturino of Bergamo, Rhenish spirituality is not the same as Tuscan: each has its own proper
characteristics.

In most systems of spirituality there can be found interaction of two or more influences; these are usually the influence of the founder of a religious order, who also leaves a heritage of certain observances to his spiritual children, and national influence, by which I mean the influence of a people's great writers rather than that of "racial" temperament. If we try to find some homogeneity in a nation's spirituality by bearing ever so little on one of these influences, the other is bound to come in and upset it. The influence of a religious founder is particularly strong, as we can soon see by comparing the most appealing Franciscan texts, the anonymous little *Indica mihi*, for instance, with the older Carthusian authors. Indeed, this is so weighty a factor that some people hold that the whole Low-Countries spirituality is comprised in Hadewijch, Ruysbroeck and the Brethren of the Common Life, all the other writers getting theirs from abroad. But again, yet other people find so great divergences between Ruysbroeck and the Brethren of the Common Life that they claim them to represent two different systems, the first speculative and concentrating on mystical experience, the second practical and concerned with what was later to be called the ascetic life.

As for the influence of great national authors, the one that matters so far as the Low Countries are concerned is obviously Ruysbroeck, and it will doubtless be remarked at once that his name is very embarassing for our argument. Everyone knows that for years Ruysbroeck has been given a place in anthologies of German mysticism, by Father Denifle[8], Dean Inge[9] and Chuzeville[10] among others, and Pourrat[11] deals with him in the chapter that he devotes to medieval German mystics. To deprive Low-Land spirituality of Ruysbroeck would be a blow from which it could hardly recover. And indeed it does seem to us that there is a tendency to over-estimate his kinship with the spirituality of the Rhineland. The Rhenish mystics did not introduce exemplarism, any more than they were the first to emphasize the mystical resources of introversion. Among neoplatonists exemplarism was a commonplace of teachers for centuries, while such men as Isaac of Stella (d. 1169) and Alger of Clairvaux (d. 1153) were familiar with the chief elements which introversion was to use a little later. If then we must vigorously refuse to hand Ruysbroeck over to the Rhenish school, it is not because of his intrinsic worth, which would be a poor enough argument anyway; but because his work was as closely bound up with that of his predecessors as with that of those that followed him. It may be objected that before his first writings he could not have become the unifying force in the spirituality of the Low Countries. But it must be remembered that he was the outcome of a process that had been going on for centuries: Hadewijch was a forerunner of Ruysbroeck just as St Albert the Great was of St Thomas Aquinas. If Ruysbroeck is to be left to the Rhenish school, then we have got to forget those unequivocal passages in which, fifty years before Master Eckhart, Hadewijch spoke of introversion and of our pre-real life in God. With his known "architectural" ability, Ruysbroeck made into an ordered system all that was best in the spirituality of the Low Countries at the end of the fourteenth century; his own contribution thereto was the pivot on which it all turned: and this was his legacy to those who came after. The mystical synthesis thus educed from the work of his predecessors, and far surpassed in the making, can be summed up as a trinitarian exemplarism which attains consciousness thanks to introversion, and blossoms into that union of the soul with the Triune God that Ruysbroeck called the "common life".

Understood in this way by good exponents of his work, Ruysbroeck's spirituality gave to a group of writers—called by some the Flemish school—the doctrinal *credo* of which they stood in need; and surely this is as good as saying that without Ruysbroeck Low-Countries spirituality would have been ns more than a body without a head. For centuries he would seem to have been its principle of cohesion, even outside the walls of the upper room where John van Leeuwen, Denis van Rijkel, Francis Vervoort and the rest were initiated into the deep places of mystical theology by their venerated master. The fact that the very practical spirituality of the Brethren of the Common Life owed so much to this master of speculative spirituality provokes thought. At their highest point the seemingly most distant groups join the speculative writers, Henry Herp and Denis the Carthusian and the rest, in a common dependence on Ruysbroeck. This or that work, the anonymous *Indica mihi* for instance, may seem completely free from this influence. But is that enough to disprove that the spirit of Ruysbroeck was a principle of cohesion in the mystical literature of the Low Countries, when it was so strong among other writers? So far as the divergence is a matter of the subjects treated by different authors, we do not think it is. A foreign writer, such as John de Saint-Samson, may appear to owe more to Ruysbroeck than some native writers. But does that prove Ruysbroeck's spirit is a very inadequate principle of demarcation of Low-Countries spirituality? Surely to say so is to do in the history of spirituality what William Lübke, Max Rooses and Andrew Michel did in the history of painting. And in any case the geographical unity that may be sufficient for art history can be shown to be not enough to mark out the domain of a spirituality.

What does it all come to ? Have we not looked for more in Father Huijben's investigation than it can give? Is it not the fact that, for lack of a preliminary definition of the meaning of the terms used, Father Huijben's conclusions have alarmed some of his readers—including ourselves?

There are two ways of understanding spirituality. For some people it is simply a reasonably definite programme of teaching. And it can be readily agreed that, looked at from this point of

view, there were at least half-a-dozen schools of spirituality
in the Low Countries, and nobody will be more successful
than Father Huijben in finding a common denominator for
them. After all, confining ourselves to the doctrinal field, what
is the common denominator of Gerson and Port-Royal, St
Francis de Sales and Madame Guyon?—yet they are all part
of French spirituality.

But spirituality can also be understood as a religious atmosphere which is not a result solely of the teaching of the different
mystics. For those who think thus, the originality of a spirituality no more consists in its exclusion of outside influences
than the originality of a writer consists in ignoring other
writers. Did St Teresa of Avila belong less to Spanish spirituality after she had, through the medium of Francis de Osuna's
*Tercer Abecedario*, felt the influence of Mauburnus (John
Mombaer) and of Thomas a Kempis—to say nothing of
Ruysbroeck? And what about Bérulle, who was a legatee of the
authoress of the *Gospel Pearl* and also the father of what
Bremond has called the "French school"? Spiritual originality
is more a matter of orientation than of a thorough independence, and in any case this last quality is nearly always decep-
tive. In time as in space, Christian mystical literature is a chain
whose links, the various writers, are the first to admit their
dependence on one another.

In spite of there being certain differences of sensibility and
emphasis, it seems to us that the influence of Ruysbroeck
himself is sufficiently pervasive to constitute that atmosphere which is as necessary to a Low-Country spirituality
as to any other. This does not mean, however, that writers
who in one way or another show characteristics of the religious
order to which they belong should be looked on as refractory,
or as foreign to the spirituality of their country. Seeing that
our Benedictines, our Carthusians, our Franciscans and others
add to what they have received from their founders certain

elements originating in Ruysbroeck, it can hardly be denied that his influence extended to these groups as well. That influence accounts for the combination of metaphysics with a piety that is often moving; and their respective proportions depend on the spirit of the times in which the writers lived as well as on their degree of attachment to the example of their holy founders. In the Low Countries, groups apparently most diverse are held together by that venerated teacher John van Ruysbroeck; it is his influence that is the common denominator or, if it be preferred, the source of the national unity, of the spirituality of the Low Countries of the old days.

## REFERENCES

[1] *Y a-t-il une spiritualité flamande?*, in *La Vie Spirituelle*, t.L. (1937), pp. [129]–[147].

[2] Paris; Tournai, 1923. (English trans.).

[3] *Les mystiques flamands et le renouveau catholique français* (Lille, 1928).

[4] This is related in a manuscript at Berne, near Heeswijk, cited by Dr H. T. Heijman in *Ons Geestelijk Erf*, t. II (1928), pp. 41–2.

[5] *Ortus et decursus Ordinis Cartusiensis*, ed. Vermeer (Wageningen, 1929), pp. 140, 21–4.

[6] *Formula brevis introductoria in vitam internam vel contemplativam*, ed Verschueren in *Tekstuitgaven van Ons Geestelijk Erf*, fasc. 1-2, t. II (Antwerp, 1931), p. 13, 199–202.

[7] The texts of this writer concerning the temperament of the various provinces of the former Low Countries were all reproduced in *Ons Geestelijk Erf*, t.I. (1927) pp. 56–60. But they are not the only ones: see James de Vitry, *Libri duo quorum prior orientalis sive hierosolymitanae; alter occidentalis historiae nomine inscribitur* (Douai, 1597), lib. II, cap. 7, p. 279.

[8] *Das Geistliche Leben, eine Blumenlese aus den Deutschen Mystikern des XIV Jahrunderts* (Graz, 1873).

[9] *Light, Life and Love, Selections from the German Mystics of the Middle Ages* (London, 1904).

[10] *Les Mystiques allemands du XIIIe au XIXe siècle* (Paris, 1935).

[11] *Christian Spirituality* (London, 1953), vol. II, pp. 224 ff.